Knock
Your
Socks
Off
Service
Recovery

Be sure to take a look at the other books in AMACOM's
bestselling Knock Your Socks Off Service series too!

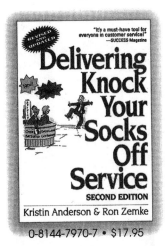

"It's a must-have tool for everyone in customer service!"
—SUCCESS Magazine

Delivering Knock Your Socks Off Service
SECOND EDITION

Kristin Anderson & Ron Zemke

0-8144-7970-7 • $17.95

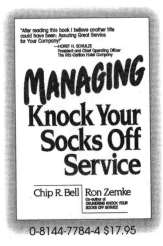

"After reading this book I believe another title could have been: Assuring Great Service for Your Company!"
—HORST H. SCHULZE
President and Chief Operating Officer
The Ritz-Carlton Hotel Company

MANAGING Knock Your Socks Off Service

Chip R. Bell | Ron Zemke
Co-author of
DELIVERING KNOCK YOUR
SOCKS OFF SERVICE

0-8144-7784-4 $17.95

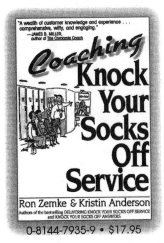

"A wealth of customer knowledge and experience . . . comprehensive, witty, and engaging."
—JAMES B. MILLER,
author of The Corporate Coach

Coaching Knock Your Socks Off Service

Ron Zemke & Kristin Anderson
Authors of the bestselling DELIVERING KNOCK YOUR SOCKS OFF SERVICE
and KNOCK YOUR SOCKS OFF ANSWERS

0-8144-7935-9 • $17.95

THOMAS K. CONNELLAN and RON ZEMKE

SUSTAINING Knock Your Socks Off SERVICE

0-8144-7824-7 • $17.95

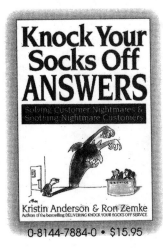

Knock Your Socks Off ANSWERS
Solving Customer Nightmares &
Soothing Nightmare Customers

Kristin Anderson & Ron Zemke
Authors of the bestselling DELIVERING KNOCK YOUR SOCKS OFF SERVICE

0-8144-7884-0 • $15.95

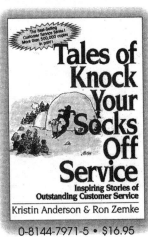

The Best-Selling
Customer Service Series!
More than 500,000 copies
in print!

Tales of Knock Your Socks Off Service
Inspiring Stories of
Outstanding Customer Service

Kristin Anderson & Ron Zemke

0-8144-7971-5 • $16.95

Available at your local bookstore, or call 1-800-262-9699.

Knock Your Socks Off Service Recovery

Ron Zemke
and Chip R. Bell

AMACOM
American Management Association
New York • Atlanta • Boston • Chicago • Kansas City • San Francisco • Washington, D.C.
Brussels • Mexico City • Tokyo • Toronto

Special discounts on bulk quantities of AMACOM books are available to corporations, professional associations, and other organizations. For details, contact Special Sales Department, AMACOM, a division of American Management Association, 1601 Broadway, New York, NY 10019.
Tel.: 212-903-8316. Fax: 212-903-8083.
Web site: www. amanet.org

This publication is designed to provide accurate and authoritative information in regard to the subject matter covered. It is sold with the understanding that the publisher is not engaged in rendering legal, accounting, or other professional service. If legal advice or other expert assistance is required, the services of a competent professional person should be sought.

Library of Congress Cataloging-in-Publication Data

Zemke, Ron.
   Knock your socks off service recovery / Ron Zemke, Chip R. Bell.
     p.   cm
   ISBN 0-8144-7084-X
   1. Customer services. 2. Customer relations. I. Bell, Chip R. II. Title.
HF5415.5   Z4595 2000
   658.8'12—dc21   00–025065

Printing number

10   9   8   7   6   5   4   3   2   1

Contents

Part One   Dollars and Sense of Service Recovery   5

Part Two   The Service Recovery Process   37

Part Three   Creating a Strategic Service Recovery System   71

7-10-00

Our Thanks

There has never been and never will be a *Knock Your Socks Off Service* book that is the product of a single mind, set of hands, or isolated creative act—or that has written itself. All eight of them—and the various revisions and updates as well—are the product of team effort. Sometimes the New York Yankees, occasionally the Keystone Kops, but a team effort no less. And a fun one. That means there are a lot of thank-yous and kudos to pass around.

David Zielinski was our Minneapolis editor and a stabilizing influence on the project. He knew all too well when we had written the same chapter for the fourth time and should move the needle into a different groove. His grasp of our ideas and aims was superb. And he was more than up to the task of finding great examples from the primordial soup of our research when our brains had turned to tapioca mush.

Jill Applegate not only typed the manuscript over and over again, but inadvertently earned a working masters degree in project management. She's still the only one who knows where all of the pieces are.

John Bush continues to amaze us with his creative illustrations and his ability to combine whimsy with truth.

Ellen Kadin, our AMACOM acquisitions editor, once again exhibited stoic calm amid the swells of craziness and cotton candy deadlines we created.

Very, very special thank-yous for Susan Zemke and Nancy Rainey Bell who, amid the hectic swirl of their own work, had the time and energy to pass out the aspirin and ego cookies in ample dosage.

Finally, we thank the many clients, colleagues, and workshop participants who gave us the opportunity to test and refine the ideas and techniques in this book.

Ron Zemke
Chip R. Bell
January 2000

Knock
Your
Socks
Off
Service
Recovery

Introduction

The Art of Service Recovery:

Fixing Broken Customers and Keeping Them on Your Side

The acid test of service quality is how you solve customers' problems.

—Leonard Berry
Texas A&M University

In a perfect world of perfect products and performances, service recovery would be a nonsensical idea. But ours is not a perfect world. It is, rather, a world filled with the mythical Dr. Murphy's gremlins. And whether you are serving customers face to face, over the phone, or via the Internet, these customers expect—and demand—redress when things go wrong.

To the customer, the true test of an organization's commitment to service quality is not the stylishness of the pledges in its marketing literature, it is the way the organization responds when things go wrong.

Service recovery is a focused effort by a service provider to return aggrieved customers to a state of satisfaction with the institution after a service or product breakdown. Note carefully the phrase "to a state of satisfaction with the institution." Any customer contact person worth his or her salt can mollify an annoyed customer and calm a screaming, ranting, and raving one in short order. You have no doubt heard some version of this refrain from a self-preservation savvy service representative, "Oh, I know, it's just terrible. If it was up to me, I'd give you your money back right now, but *they've* got this policy and if I break it, well—you know!" That gets the service rep off the hook with the customer but does little to endear or retain the customer for the organization. Service recovery is about keeping customers coming back after disaster strikes or even if just something annoying happens. In simple terms, recovery is the special effort customers expect you to put forward when things have gone a little—or a lot—wrong for them.

Effective service recovery that saves at-risk customers for the organization and becomes a competitive distinguisher is not an accident or a random act of will. It is, rather, a planned, systematic process. An effective service recovery system is more than an elaborate apology and monetary make-good effort designed to mollify upset customers, curry their favor, and, if necessary, buy back their business. The core attributes of an effective service recovery system are a clear problem-resolution process, a complaint and problem capture and analysis subsystem, and a way of feeding information on systematic problems back into the system to help reduce their occurrence. At the same time, effective recovery is a set of skillful, real-time actions taken by carefully selected individuals who are trained in the tact and diplomacy necessary to successfully manage an upset, disappointed, or frightened customer. Successful recovery is the perfect blend of carefully thought-out processes and procedures and skillful, often spontaneous, actions. When done well, it can help right even the most grievous wrongs and save customers who already are one step out the door toward the competition.

About This Book

This book is designed and written for supervisors and managers who are responsible for hiring, training, coaching, and motivating customer contact employees who deal with upset, disappointed, unhappy customers. Consider it a handbook to help employees help customers and keep them coming back even when those customers have experienced problems with the products and services of your organization.

There are five sections to this book:

- The *Dollars and Sense of Service Recovery* chapters look at the economics of recovery, what it costs to lose and save "at-risk" customers, and the return on investment from creating effective recovery systems. It is your "argument" for spending time and money to create teams that can deliver first-class recovery.
- The *Service Recovery Process* chapters focus on service recovery in action. This section is a schematic of the steps customer service representatives and other employees can take face to face, ear to phone, or keyboard to computer screen to deal successfully with real-time, upset customers. It is a highly flexible, easy to learn, but very robust system we have developed from 15 years of researching and consulting on effective customer saving service recovery.
- The *Creating A Strategic Service Recovery System* section is about what goes on beneath the line of visibility—the parts of the recovery operation the customer never sees—that make it possible for your highly trained, carefully selected front-line service pros to make recovery look easy, natural, and effortless. The core of the strategic service re-

covery system is the rules, policies and procedures, and service improvement processes that make it an integral part of your management system.

- The *Leading Service Recovery* chapters look carefully at the leadership role management must exert and exhibit if recovery efforts are to be a successful, sustained part of your organization's customer relationship management effort. Included are tips and techniques for finding, training, coaching, and retaining people with first-class service recovery and customer relations skills.
- The fifth and final section, The *Service Recovery Toolkit,* is just that, a soup-to-nuts toolkit for building an effective service recovery capability and a ready guide for you to use to help employees brush up on their recovery skills. Included is an assessment instrument to determine your current level of service recovery readiness.

The "Rules" of First-Class Customer Care

- Rule One in effective customer service is "always do it right the first time." Whether "it" is fixing the car, shipping the product, or solving a customer problem, your systems, policies, and practices should strive to make you "easy to do business with" in your customers' eyes. It should be your platinum standard.
- Rule Two is do it very, very right when things have gone wrong for the customer. And to do the "fixing" without leaving the customer with a bad taste or the memory of a nightmare experience.
- Rule Three is that most customers do not give you a third chance . . . they simply walk away. And never come back. Ever. And they tell others how bad you are. And blemish your reputation in the marketplace.

This book is about making the most of those precious second chances customers give you for redemption and retention. Making the most of those opportunities keeps them coming back and on your side, even when the worst has happened.

Part One

Dollars and Sense of Service Recovery

If you have trouble, it reduces the likelihood that the person is going to buy the next time.

—Joseph M. Juran
Founding father of Quality Control

At the core of every commercial contract and social compact is a promise. Keep that promise and everyone profits and comes away from the transaction a little bit better for the effort.

But fall short and all manner of bad things can happen—for everyone concerned. There are direct and indirect economic consequences for buyer and seller, giver and receiver. Customers who feel cheated demand their money back and swear never to do business with you again. And they warn others to stay clear of you.

5

Fix the problem; commit an act of effective service recovery; do it faster, better, and with less imposition on the customer than he or she had dreaded, and they sing your praises. And come back. And trust you anew. They have seen you at your best, and they know it. Service recovery is the art of fixing what went wrong for the customer and mending the damage that error, mistake, or misstep did to your relationship with the customer. Service recovery is about restoring trust when your customer is most vulnerable to doubt.

1

The Economics of Service Recovery

He who gives great service gets great returns.

—Elbert Hubbard
Nineteenth-century American writer

The numbers are in and the case airtight: Companies that perform high-quality service recovery realize substantial economic payoff. According to John Goodman, president of Technical Assistance Research Programs, Inc. (TARP), an Arlington, Virginia-based market research firm,[1] studies conducted by TARP over the last 5 years all found that when customers' problems were satisfactorily handled and resolved, their loyalty and repurchase intentions were within a few percentage points of those customers who had not experienced a product or service failure.

Even more intriguing are four other TARP studies that surveyed, respectively, industrial customers of a Canadian chemical company, high-value customers of an American bank, customers of two global computer companies, and professional photographers who were customers of a European photographic supply company. These studies found that customers whose complaints were quickly satisfied were more likely to purchase additional products than even those customers who experienced no problems with the organization or its products (Figure 1-1). In

---

1. John Goodman, "Don't Fix the Product, Fix the Customer," *Quality Review,* Fall 1988: 8–11.

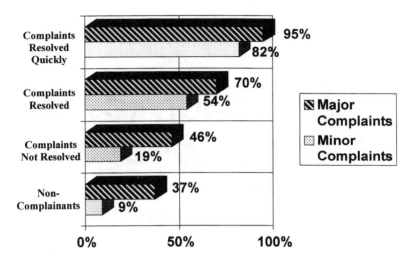

Reproduced with permission from TARP, "Don't Fix the Product, Fix the Customer," *Quality Review*, Fall 1988: 8–11.

Figure 1-1. How many of your unhappy customers will buy from you again?

the United States, a camera manufacturer found that customers who telephoned to ask about or report problems with camera gear "can be sold additional photographic equipment once the subject of the call has been handled to the customer's satisfaction."[2] This finding casts substantial doubt on the commonly held notion that a high-visibility service recovery effort is always a loss leader. It can, in fact, be a direct profit generator.

In other words, TARP's research strongly suggests that swift and effective service recovery enhances customers' perception of the quality of the products and services they have already purchased, as well as their perception of the competence of the organization and its personnel. This also enhances the perceived quality and value of other products and services the organization offers.

Leonard L. Berry, professor of marketing and director of the Center of Retailing Studies at Texas A&M University and one of the leading service quality researchers in the United States, is

2. Ibid.

equally adamant about the importance of good service recovery, "The acid test of service quality is how you solve customer problems."[3] And though he is cautious, if not skeptical, about Goodman's finding that good recovery can lead to better than average customer loyalty, he is very sure that the quality of recovery the customer experiences when things go wrong has a strong impact on overall customer satisfaction and customer retention.

In a series of studies conducted over the past 10 years, Berry and colleagues Valarie A. Zeithaml and A. Parasuraman consistently found that the best customer satisfaction scores come from customers who experienced no problems, the second best from those whose problems were resolved satisfactorily, and the worst from customers whose problems remained unsolved. Those differences are statistically and practically significant. The message from all this research is clear: Get service right the first time. If you do not, be darned sure you do it right the second time. If you fail—if you do not meet the customer's expectations twice—that is about all the room the customer will give you.[4]

Using research models similar to those that TARP, and Berry and his colleagues use, individual businesses are learning on their own about the impact effective service recovery can have on their customers. Research at Minneapolis-based National Car Rental, for example, found that although there is an 85 percent chance that a satisfied customer will rent again from National, there is a 90 percent probability that a customer who experienced great service recovery will rent again.[5]

A large, midwest-based U.S. hotel corporation studied the bottom-line fallout from guests who have problems that are not satisfactorily resolved. Operation researchers at the company took into account the average number of room nights per year per frequent business travel customer (the largest and most desirable segment of its customer base), the number of other travelers that an unhappy guest will influence to avoid its properties,

3. Chip R. Bell and Ron Zemke, "Service Recovery: Doing It Right the Second Time," *Training Magazine,* June 1990: 42–48.
4. Ibid.
5. Jean M. Otte, corporate vice president of quality management, National Car Rental System, Inc., presentation to MN Chapter, Society of Consumer Affairs Professionals in Business, June 8, 1992.

the acquisition cost for that original traveler, and the marketing costs involved in replacing that traveler if he or she decides never to use any of its properties again. Although the exact calculations are proprietary, this corporation believes that the net loss value of one frequent business traveler guest is equivalent to 81 room nights or $6,480.00.[6]

Understanding the dollar impact of losing and replacing a customer is a critical first step to making service recovery an important strategic tool for your customer service operation. The impact of poor recovery goes beyond the loss of a single customer. The salesperson or customer service rep who dismisses an unhappy or complaining customer with a perfunctory "I can't help you, that's our policy" positions the company to lose dozens, if not hundreds, of current and potential customers. The problem, as the case of the hotel company so clearly illustrates, is that complaining customers do not simply go away. They go away, stay away, and, worse yet, take every opportunity to tell anyone who will listen about the rotten treatment they had to endure at the hands of your company. Call it the "grapevine effect." People relish in telling others about the rotten treatment they received at the hands of their local laundry, grocery, bank, or fill-in-the-blank corporate company. No dinner party or coffee break gathering with four or more friends is complete without a rendition of the tune, "You won't believe how long I was on hold with Acme software trying to make my computer work this time!"

Several independent studies confirmed that although 50 percent of upset customers will complain to the organization's local outlets, as many as 96 percent of unhappy customers will not complain to the head office of the offending business or the manufacturer, but they will tell, on average, nine to ten friends, acquaintances, or colleagues how bad your service is. One study we conducted found that 18 percent of customers were upset with treatment they received at the hands of a midwestern

6. This research was initiated by an executive of the hotel corporation as part of a service management operations course at a local university. The corporation now uses these data to justify making the bottom 5 percent of its franchises (as determined by CSI) "available to the industry." They simply cannot afford to keep properties and personnel that drive away customers.

phone company. These upset customers reported they each told, on average, twenty or more people of their plight. According to a study conducted by General Electric, word of mouth has a significant impact on sales as well. The General Electric study found that "the impact of word of mouth on a customer's repurchase decision is twice as important as corporate advertising."[7]

Indeed, John Goodman, of the TARP research group, believes organizations regularly miss opportunities to capitalize on powerful and cost-effective word-of-mouth advertising available from simply "surprising" customers with effective recovery. Goodman has advocated that companies reallocate up to 10 percent of their mass media advertising budgets to improve customer service. When he made this suggestion a few years ago while speaking before an advertising trade group, he got the predictable public response, "But Sir, that is irretrievable over-

7. J. Goodman et al., "Setting Priorities for Satisfaction Improvement," in *Service Wisdom: Creating and Maintaining the Customer Service Edge*, eds. Ron Zemke and Chip R. Bell (Minneapolis: Lakewood Books, 1990). First published in the *Quality Review*, Winter 1987.

head!" Later, a number of the more savvy and progressive corporate advertising directors attending the meeting pulled him aside privately to tell him he was "right on," and they had the data to prove it.

The damage done via traditional word of mouth is modest compared to what happens today on the Internet. With today's technology, bad service experiences now travel at warp speed and to far corners on the globe. Traditionally, a disgruntled customer might tell five to ten people about her unhappy service experience on a one-to-one basis. Now, however, thanks to web chat groups, bulletin boards, online user groups, and broadcast e-mail, the medium of choice for venting upset with a company has become one-to-many. Frustrated or angry customers can deliver a screenful of damaging information about your company to hundreds or even thousands in an instant. There are even web sites operated by specific consumer advocacy groups that solicit reports of poor customer service and disappointing experiences with company and agency products and service. One of the strongest, most visited sites chronicles the complaints and woes of commercial travelers (*www.passengerrights.com*). Oh, and don't think the competition does not use those posted rantings and ravings to study your weaknesses and look for vulnerabilities.

A few years ago, Sony got a taste of Internet information whiplash when a computer scientist for the National Institute of Standards and Technology took offense to a Sony ad that ran on MTV. In the scientist's view, the ad was extremely sexist and deserving of comment. She took her protest, via an electronic bulletin board, to members of Syster, a group composed of some 1,500 women in the field of computer operating systems research. After describing the commercial, the scientist declared over the e-waves that she would not purchase any Sony products until the commercial was withdrawn from the air. In an interview with the *Wall Street Journal*, she sounded a sterner warning, "An electronic bulletin board can mobilize a grassroots movement within hours, and the collective outrage can be focused at individual companies." The commercial was soon pulled from the air.

Although such consumer protests can create a stir, the real damage is done in business-to-business or tightly niched, narrowly focused operations. Sample, for instance, the harping that goes on in bulletin boards and chat rooms where people discuss computer hardware, software, or service support issues. People writing these scathing commentaries are not corporate lightweights. Many are charged with making repurchase decisions for their companies.

Frederick Reichheld of Bain and Co. and W. Earl Sasser of Bain of Harvard University have taken the TARP findings one step further.[8] They calculated the value of customer retention over a 5-year period for nine industries. Like TARP, they considered not only base profit but profit from increased purchases, profit from reduced operating costs (attainable through increased knowledge of a customer's requirements over time), profits from word-of-mouth referrals, and profits from price premium purchases. Reichheld and Sasser found that profits from a single customer are not static but increase over time. In other words, a customer who has been with you for 5 years (depending on your industry) can be up to 377 percent more profitable than a customer you have only just wooed to your products or services. Their bottom-line calculation is that by focusing on customer retention tactics, such as service recovery and reducing annual customer defections by a mere 5 percent, an organization can boost pretax profits 25 to 125 percent.

The net learning from all this research is that focusing on service recovery pays, and it pays well. And to ignore its necessity is to count disaster for your organization.

8. Frederick Reichheld and W. Earl Sasser, "Zero Defections: Quality Comes to Services," *Harvard Business Review,* September-October 1990: 105.

2

Using Proactive Recovery to Rescue At-Risk Customers

Don't find a fault. Find a remedy.

—Henry Ford
U.S. automobile manufacturer

Service recovery traditionally has been focused on responding to complaints from customers and mollifying those who are kind enough to give you an opportunity to redeem yourself and save their business. This traditional service recovery—fixing upset customers and broken promises—works well, when and if a customer lets you know there has been a problem. Unfortunately, a growing culture of combative complaint handling is leading many customers to conclude that they would rather switch than fight. To impact these silent but at-risk customers, it is important to find ways to reach out to them with either a promise of easy redress or a process that demonstrates concern.

Gracie Golf is a pseudonym for an east coast U.S. catalog company that markets clothing and gifts to the over fifty, male and female golf enthusiast set. Gracie customers, reports Jeff McLeod of Minneapolis-based Parametrica systems, who consults with the company, are segmented into one of three classifications based on their buying behavior and service satisfaction ratings of the company:

- **Apostles.** Customers of 3 years or more who order more than $200 in goods annually, give the company high

14

marks for service, and promote Gracie goods to friends and acquaintances.

- **Satisfied Users.** Customers of 3 years or more who order $80 to $120 a year and are generally satisfied with Gracie but do not promote the company and its products to others.
- **Marginals.** Customers of 3 years and more who purchase sporadically (primarily from clearance fliers), order less than $80 a year, and give Gracie less than sterling reviews.

A detailed analysis of purchase and repurchase behavior found that many satisfied and most marginal customers also could be classified as high "at-risk" customers—buyers who could be lured away for a small price or selection differential. As a result, Gracie began packing short, bounce-back, customer sensitivity surveys with every product order. Previous research had determined that the look of Gracie's catalogs, the breadth of product selection, the customers' perception of price/value, and the customers' experience with basic service (specifically timely delivery, product return policies, and ease of credit issuance) were high-satisfaction sensitivity factors. That is, low scores on survey items pertaining to the look of the catalog, breadth of selection, price/value, and basic service almost invariably were accompanied by low scores on repurchase predictions (who would buy from Gracie again) and negative changes in actual purchasing behavior.

Rather than simply bemoan low scores on the bounce-back surveys, Gracie viewed the results as an opportunity to intervene on the customers' behalf. Specific response patterns on the surveys—those related to the sensitivity factors—now trigger a follow-up phone call to high at-risk customers from a member of a specially trained and empowered recovery crew called the retrieval squad. A squad member thanks the customer for the order and for the feedback, then probes for more detail. If a specific problem is at the root of the low rating, the rep offers an apology and discusses possible fixes for the problem. If a particular piece of clothing proves below par, the rep offers a replacement or a refund. If the problem is with, say, a discounted golf club, the rep will offer to take it back, upgrade it with a better club at a minimum cost, or give the customer a special credit against a future purchase. The recovery rep then probes for other disappointments and repairs any additional problems that come up. If two or more problems are mentioned, the rep offers the customer a gift certificate and complimentary shipping charges for his next order. The customer's name then goes on a list to receive a longer, more detailed survey at the next quarterly customer satisfaction survey interval.

In the first year of implementation, at-risk customers who were pulse called—customers who rated themselves as likely to stop doing business with Gracie—averaged $100 *more* in total annual purchases than at-risk customers who were not contacted by the retrieval squad. Because of that effort, the company realized a $2 million net improvement on a two-million client base, traceable directly to increased purchases by pulse-called, at-risk customers (Figure 2-1). Equally important, a significant percentage of the at-risk customers could be reclassified as satisfied customers after the next quarterly long-form customer satisfaction survey. That evidence in hand, the company widened

Customer Type	Average Revenue	Customer Base Year 1	Revenues Year 1 ($M)	Customer Base Year 2	Revenues Year 2 ($M)	Change Y1 to Y2
Apostles	$200	656,000	$131.2	656,000	$131.2	0%
Satisfieds	$150	1,098,000	$164.7	1,098,000	$164.7	0%
Marginals	$50	246,000	$12.3	226,000	$11.3	-1%
Retrievals	$150	-	-	20,000	$3.0	-+
		2,000,000	$308.2 M	2,000,000	$310.2 M	+0.6%

Figure 2-1. Revenue by customer classification.

the pulse-calling effort to include not only at-risk but marginally satisfied customers as well.

Gracie is not the only company that is proactive in identifying and saving at-risk customers. Others see the wisdom and bottom-line payoff of taking preemptive steps to ensure customers who have experienced problems large or small stay in the fold. A few examples follow.

"CAR Pooling" At-Risk Customers at MCI

Although popular wisdom says recovery efforts most prudently are spent on large, high-margin customers, the reality is the largest single identifiable group of customers for many business-to-business operations is small business, not companies of the Fortune 500 roster. Recovery for the small guy's problems pays, too. MCI WorldCom refers to a small customer with a sudden case of chronic breakdown and disappointment as a customer at risk (CAR). In the past, these customers became immediate candidates for "CAR pooling," or extra special handling and attention by service personnel.

The CAR pool process begins when a customer with a history of "troubles" is nominated as a CAR pool candidate by a front-line service person or supervisor. Quality assurance and customer service managers review the nomination and assign a CAR pool "driver" to the customer. Every one of the sixty-plus employees of the quality assurance and customer service staff is eligible for a driver assignment. The driver's key role is expedition: to drive the rest of the organization to find a permanent fix to the customer's recurring problem. The driver is expected to look for root causes, create a plan for a permanent resolution, and stay on top of the situation. In addition, the driver immediately opens a dialogue with the customer, establishes himself or herself as the key contact, and assures the customer that a special investigation is under way.

Other departments understand that solving at-risk customer problems is to be given priority and that CAR pool drivers are to be cooperated with. Although CAR pool assignments are given top priority, they are distributed as additional workload—

and on an alphabetical basis—within the quality assurance and customer service departments.

The concept, which emerged from a front-line employee problem-solving group, proved a hit with customers and employees alike. "Customers are surprised by the attention," Kim Charlesworth, then an MCI senior manager for quality assurance, told *The Service Edge Newsletter*, " because they're used to being treated as second-class citizens by big businesses. Some have even increased the business they do with us based on the extra effort they see placed on solving their problems."

Chase "Babies" At-Risk Customers Back

Customers behind on their credit card payments can expect the usual strong-arm tactics: ominous warning letters or threatening phone calls. But rather than risk losing these delinquent customers altogether in highly competitive markets, some banks turned to kinder and gentler approaches to get these customers back on track.

According to the *Associated Press*, the banks experimented with mailing "we feel your pain" videotapes that implore the customers to confer with a credit officer and set up reasonable repayment schedules. Tapes sent by Chase Manhattan Corp., for instance, featured an actor playing a bank representative who says, "Together, we can work it out," and the tape repeatedly urged delinquents to call an 800 number on the screen. Customers who call the bank are treated with dignity and not raked over the coals, claimed the 7-minute video, which AP says cost the bank $37,000 to produce and $3.50 each to mail.

Chase opted to try the videos nationwide after a pilot test with 10,000 west coast customers improved collections. The bank sent the video to select cardholders who had not paid their bills in 3 months and were not responding to repeated phone calls.

The result? Chase heard from 28 percent more people than before the videos were sent. Credit counselors say the videotape strategy is not necessarily a public relations gimmick; people who owe money often are depressed and have lost some pride.

The tapes help get them to respond because it is a different, more customer-friendly approach, they say.

Muzak Tunes into At-Risk Customers

Muzak, the Seattle-based provider of business music systems, created a process to identify "customers at risk" and then work to keep their business. The company's Customer Contact Program (CCP) uses a six-step process to stay on top of customer complaints before they result in lost contracts. First, contract cancellation rates are determined for affiliate offices, and targets are set for surveying customers. Customer contact reps conduct phone surveys and divide customers into "satisfied" and "dissatisfied" groups, and the findings are forwarded to the appropriate department for corrective action.

Within a week of the rep's initial contact, dissatisfied customers are contacted to resolve any service, equipment, or administrative problems they may have referenced in the phone

call. If they request a change in music, a Muzak salesperson comes to their aid.

The program targeted customers whose contracts would expire in 24 months. As a result of the at-risk retention efforts, more contacted subscribers are not only staying with Muzak, company executives told *The Service Edge Newsletter*, they are increasing their services by an average of one-third when they renew contracts. The program contributed to a 28 percent decrease in subscriber cancellations in its first year.

The Moral of the Story

One of us, after a history of several months of discontent, recently changed cell-phone service providers. Within days, a representative of the company called to inquire about the cancellation. After a recitation of the problems that precipitated the move, the customer rep whined back, "But you should have let us know you were *that* upset." In today's high-pressure, must-perform environment, it is not the customer's responsibility to tell you recovery is needed. It is your challenge to be ahead of and look for ways to prevent those at-risk customers from folding their cards and walking away in search of a better game.

Estimating Your At-Risk Ratio

The best way to measure and understand your at-risk customer base is to follow Gracie Golf's example and build a survey and customer call-back system. That is our view anyway.

At the very least, a sensitive, predictive survey system is a must. That said, it is useful to attempt to estimate your current at-risk customer base. Estimating will give you a general sense of your at-the-moment, at-risk position.

This estimating revolves around filling in the blanks in the "tree" in Figure 2-2. The tree is based on data from a variety of sources, including Performance Research Associates and TARP. Here is how it works.

At-Risk Customer Guesstimator

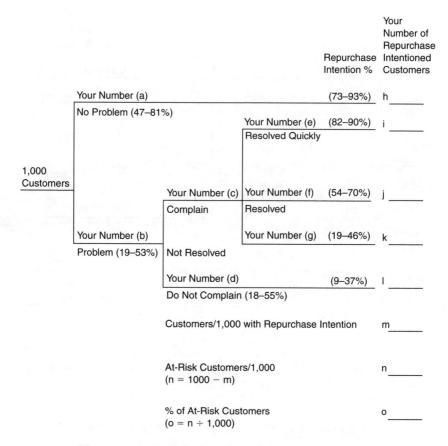

Figure 2-2. Gracie Golf at-risk rescue results.

1. The calculation begins with a hypothetical pod of 1,000 customers. The first branching of the tree is to separate these theoretical 1,000 customers into two groups: customers who have experienced a problem with your product or service (b) and customers who have not (a). You do this by reasoned windage. Our data suggest that between 47 and 81 percent of customers will have experienced no problem with your product or service. It is up to you to decide where your organization falls in this spectrum.

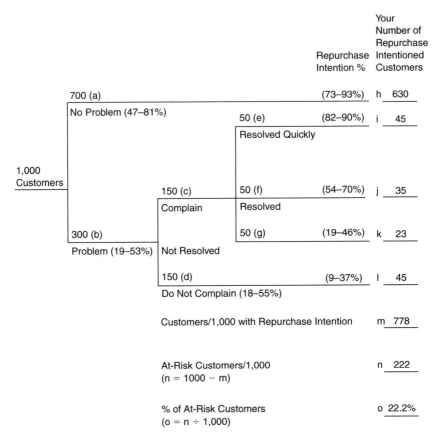

Figure 2-3. At-risk customer Guesstimator.

In the example shown in Figure 2-3, we used 70 percent. That means that 700 of the 1,000 customers in the hypothetical customer pod would tell us they have never had a problem with Acme Inc.

2. This step is dead simple. Fill in line (b) with the difference between 1,000 and whatever you put in the parentheses at (a). For Acme Inc., that comes to 300 customers.

3. Now it gets a little tricky. One of two things can happen with customers who have a problem. They can complain (c), or they can keep it to themselves (d).

Our experience with customers says that between 45 and 82 percent will complain. Again, you have to take a guess here. In the example of Acme Inc. in Figure 2-3, we went down the middle, estimating that 50 percent (150 of the 300) of the customers with problems complained; hence, the 150 in the parentheses at (c).

That also means that 150 goes on the "do not complain" line at (d).

4. Three things of significance can happen when a customer complains.

- The complaint can be resolved quickly (e).
- The complaint can be resolved but not quickly (f).
- The complaint can go unresolved (g).

Only you can guesstimate what the proper proportions are for your organization.

For our Acme Inc. example, we split the pod evenly, that is, we put fifty customers on each line.

5. Now the plot thickens. The calculations become a little trickier, but they are worth pursuing.

Line "h" is the number of "no problem" customers who will purchase from you again. Experience says between 73 and 93 percent. For Acme Inc., we went with 90 percent or 630 customers.

Lines "i," "j", and "k" are where you record repurchase likelihood for complaining customers. For Acme Inc., we used the maximum figures in the brackets, specifically 90, 70, and 46 percent. Or, in terms of actual customers who are likely to repurchase from Acme Inc.:

- Resolved quickly (i) = 45.
- Resolved (j) = 35.
- Unresolved (k) = 23.

Customers who have experienced a problem but do not complain repurchase at a rate between 9 and 37 percent. For the Acme Inc. example, we used 30 percent, just because it generates an even number. That puts 45 customers on line "l."

6. Just about done now. All that is left is to add up the far-right column, that is, lines "h" through "l," and record the sum at "m." For Acme Inc. that comes to 778.

> To figure the number of at-risk or least likely to repurchase customers, subtract line "m" from 1,000. For Acme Inc., 1,000 − 778 = 222 at-risk customers.
>
> Your at-risk proportion or percentage comes to line "n" divided by 1,000. For Acme Inc., this comes to 222 ÷ 1000 or 22.2 percent.

In short, Acme Inc., our mythical company, is at-risk with 22.2 percent of its customers. When we do this calculation with "for real" companies, using real data, the results vary from 15 to 40 percent. If your guesstimate is outside this range, you might want to go back and reexamine your assumptions and/or your math.

Figure 2-2 is a clean, unsullied version of the At-Risk Customer Guesstimator™. You have our blessing to photocopy it and use it in-house to see what sort of consensus guess you can garner by having, say, six to ten people fill it out and averaging your combined guesstimates.[1]

3

Reactivation:

The Recovery of Lost "Souls"

It's not the one thousand dollar things that upset the customer, but the five buck things that bug them.

—Earl Fletcher
Volkswagen, Canada

When most service managers think recovery, they think about saving current customers who have experienced stretches of turbulence, and that is appropriate. But what about customers who, for one reason or another, have already stopped doing business with you? Does it make sense to try to "recover" their business? To bring them back to the land of life accounts?

The experience of a growing number of businesses suggests an account reactivation effort often is time and money wisely spent.

Most organizations simply write off lost or "dead" customers and then get busy refilling the cupboards with replacements. But prospecting for new customers is among the most costly, difficult, and risky tasks in business. Dedicating some of those recruiting dollars to salvaging lost customer relationships makes sense. Unlike new prospects, past and present customers do not need to be qualified. They can provide valuable input about why they left that can help improve your company. Say there's a bump in your business processes—a product defect, a badly designed customer service process, restrictive hours, high prices—that is driving customers away. Does it make sense to write off customers driven off by those problems, or is it more economical and efficient to try to woo back those lost customers?

One approach is simply to install a focused call-back program aimed at lost customers. Federal Express has done this. One FedEx customer canceled his account when a critical international shipment containing payroll checks arrived late. FedEx investigated and found the holdup had occurred at customs; it was beyond the company's control. When a FedEx phone rep called the lost customer to explain the situation and offered tips to streamline the customer's international documentation along the way, she won back the account.

Telemarketing consultant George Walther says a FedEx sales rep called him after a telephone agent noticed his shipping activity had dramatically tapered off. Walter explained that he had shifted his business to UPS because he thought its 2-day service was cheaper. Sensing Walther slipping away, the FedEx rep scheduled a sales call to try to show him that FedEx's 2-day service was actually cheaper. Walther eventually reopened his account with FedEx, in part because of the rep's extra effort.

Restek Corp., a Bellefonte, Pennsylvania manufacturer of laboratory equipment, used a unique incentive system to help recover lost customers. The company keeps a database with four key customer groupings: new customers, customers with recent complaints, "lost" customers, and recent purchasers of additional product. According to *The Service Edge Newsletter*, Restek factory workers have volunteered their time—on breaks, during lunches, or before or after work shifts—to call these customers to check on satisfaction levels, probe for any postsale problems, and try to win back lost accounts. They are rewarded for the extra work with time that can be taken as additional pay or vacation. One or two calls per month might be worth one-quarter day's pay or vacation time, and three to five calls per week worth a 1-day award.

Calls made to "lost" customers—those who have not made a purchase in the past year—are the most immediately valuable to Restek's business. They learned that one of the reasons customers drop off is revolving-door personnel; purchasing agents or end users in client companies turn over frequently, and their replacements often are not familiar with Restek. Managers report that simply touching base with these new employees and making them aware of Restek's offerings has recaptured more than 50 percent of that old business.

Although the company might fall behind in making calls to the other three customer segments, it makes sure to stay on schedule with lost customers. "The re-up and retention rate for those lost and potentially lost customers more than justified the program's cost in bonus payouts to employees," technical marketing director Neil Moseman reports.

Calling scripts are prepared for each customer segment and phone training provided. The caller's job is to gather information and return it to a follow-up coordinator, who forwards it to the appropriate work group. Should a technical issue arise that is beyond an employee's knowledge base, the call is forwarded to one of 25 trained Restek technicians.

An important part of the goal for reactivation programs like Restek's is to find out what caused customers to go to all the trouble of leaving and establishing an entirely new vendor relationship. That is, after all, a lot of bother for an organization. Contacting "dead" customers helps you learn the whys of abandonment and provides critical feedback on your company's strengths and weaknesses. The ample byproduct is returning some of these lost customers to "current-and-paying" status.

Small Business Report magazine (August 1993) told of the owner of a cleaning services company who kept the names of 15,000 customers who had used his services at one time over the past 10 years but were no longer. These former customers had not used his services for as long as 3 years, did not return calls, or seemed to have simply vanished. The list grew quietly over the years as the company became a success. Eventually, the owner realized he was spending too much time and money chasing the business of new customers. That is when he decided to attempt to revive customers on the inactive list and refocus on creating long-term relationships. Six months later, after a forced effort to contact all 15,000 inactives by phone, the company had reactivated 22 percent. That generated $4 million in revenue.

Better yet, 80 percent of those reactivated customers continued to use his services a year later.

Phone campaigns work better than written entreaties or surveys because callers can express a high level of concern and dig for true reasons customers stopped doing business with you. But a reactivation campaign requires careful preparation. It is critical to collect as much information as possible about each account before calling. Your callers will lack credibility and reduce chances of reactivation if they do not know at least the bare essentials of a customer's history with your firm.

Callers also must be well trained to deal with the variety and intensity of responses they will likely encounter—"Your product wasn't at all what I expected," "We got it cheaper somewhere else," "The person who dealt with your account left the company," "I was insulted by your contact person"—to help convince lost customers to try your services again.

And just as Gracie Golf found that special treatment and attention was important to strengthening its bonds with "at-risk" customers, "reactivated" customers need to be put on a special treatment and attention regime. And, of course, that regime has to be cost justified based on account profitability parameters for your organization. But, at a minimum, reactivated accounts should be:

    A. Assigned the name of a contact person the customer can call with concerns.

    B. Thanked in writing for reconsideration and reassured that previously experienced problems will not recur.

    C. Called after every product delivery or service performance for the first 30 days of reactivation.

    D. Contacted at the first billing to confirm that things are proceeding according to the customer's desires.

Where should a reactivation effort reside? Some organizations vote for sales and marketing. Others prefer a specialized third party be given the nod. We respectfully disagree. We believe those who will be most involved in keeping that customer happy—the recovery experts and the customer service pros—should have the honor and opportunity to restore the lost to a state of satisfaction with the organization. And down the road, when budgets once again are tight, your success at recovery and reactivation will be an elegant testament to your organizational value.

4

The Psychology of Recovery:

Inside the Mind of a Broken Customer

When it comes to service recovery, there are three rules to keep in mind:

(1) Do it right the first time.

(2) Fix it properly if it ever fails.

(3) Remember: There are no third chances.

—Leonard Berry
Marketing Professor, Texas A&M University

All service recovery begins with an expectation of fairness. Customers enter the service experience with one or more pre-conceived ideas about what should happen to set things right. When the experience approximates the expectation, the customer is in emotional balance. Most, although certainly not all, customers assume the world will treat them fairly. This is not a mark of naiveté; it simply is a recognition that, on balance, most customers have more life experience that falls on the "fair" than on the "not fair" side of the ledger.

So when a service provider acts in a manner the customer deems unfair, customers feel betrayed, that an implied promise was not honored. What is critical to good recovery is understanding that the customer's view of the world is accurate and *reasonable from his or her point of view,* not necessarily from the viewpoint of your organization. Customers *do* make mistakes, and they know they make mistakes. But they assume their views of what should happen after a mistake is found out, whether the error was caused by they themselves or by the organization, is the only right, or reasonable, course of action. When that view is directly challenged, customers assume the challenger is both wrong and is attempting to control, prevail, coerce, or engage in all manner of unrighteous action.

Understanding customers' emotional states when events veer far off their anticipated course, when an expected right turn suddenly becomes a left, is an essential first step to returning them to a state of satisfaction. It is at this point where right or wrong begins to take a back seat, and when the customer's unique perspective on the problem at hand must be heard and understood, and, if at all possible, honored.

This is the "sense"—the customer logic—that accompanies and fuels the dollars of effective service recovery.

The Case of Mrs. Dewey

Take Mrs. Dewey, a retired librarian living alone on a fixed income. Widowed, she has bootstrapped her way to financial competence after her husband's passing, spending long hours educating herself on the ledger book, insurance policies, health care plans, and tax returns.

But 3 months in a row now, Mrs. Dewey's bank has overstated her balance, causing her to assume she had more funds than she actually had. Three times she has been called by local merchants complaining of a bounced check. Each time Mrs. Dewey has walked to the nearest branch of her bank and haggled for over an hour with a service assistant, finally succeeding in getting this junior officer to acknowledge the error and grudgingly call the involved merchants to restore her good credit.

When it happened again for a fourth time—another overstatement, another bounced check—Mrs. Dewey drew the line. This time Mrs. Dewey waited in line for 20 minutes only to be told by another customer service representative she would have to see the branch manager and not tie up the customer service counter line. And, by the way, the manager would be out to lunch with the regional vice president for at least another hour.

"They don't get it!" Mrs. Dewey said loudly as she stalked out of the branch. She was speaking to no one and feeling everyone in the bank had purposely let her down.

Journey to the Center of an Aggrieved Mind

Previously, Mrs. Dewey had dealt with bank employees who had given her the benefit of the doubt, assumed her description of a problem was accurate, and worked to help unravel the situation. During this latest series of snafus, however, the institution had fallen far short of her expectations or her preconceived notions of what should happen when she presents a problem to the bank. Those expectations had been dashed hard against the jagged rocks of organizational indifference and condescension and destroyed her confidence, perhaps for good.

When the customer service representative initially viewed Mrs. Dewey's interpretation of her financial papers as inaccurate, Mrs. Dewey moved to defend her "correct" point of view. When she eventually was proved right, it affirmed her perception that the bank's actions were not on her behalf and probably were calculated to make her life difficult. Her trust was severely eroded. She subconsciously vowed to stay on guard and be more forceful if ever again challenged. Each recurrence further eroded her trust of the bank and her tolerance.

Mrs. Dewey received repeated reinforcement of her view that the bank had acted "unjustly" and was not interested in being "fair" to her. And her situation was complicated by an additional factor. The service encounter threatened her livelihood. Her reputation depended on her credit.

When customers' sense of well being is threatened or a key value, such as fairness, freedom, or security, is challenged, they move away from rational behavior, eventually adopting an adversarial, "take no prisoners" stance regarding relations with the organization. When customers who have been pushed to anger encounter indifference, their reaction is as predictable as a match in a pool of gasoline. At this stage of a potential recovery scenario, the provoked customer finds a ho-hum, indifferent response from the service provider that is puzzling beyond comprehension, as in Mrs. Dewey's "They don't get it!"

The Lessons of Mrs. Dewey: A Revisionist View

What lessons can be learned by understanding this "psychology of recovery," by hitching a ride aboard the customer's psyche as it journeys through the emotionally volatile land of service breakdown? How could the bank have managed Mrs. Dewey's exasperating experience toward a more positive outcome?

- **Lesson One.** Assume the customers' view of their situation is absolutely accurate—from their side of the transaction. Read that sentence again. It is not about their view. It is about their "view of their view." Whether the customer is right or wrong is not relevant. In fact, focusing on "who gets to be right" is potentially harmful to the long-term health of the relationship. Focus instead on problem solving and moving toward collective discovery, not accusations and proof of your "rightness." Even if you are ultimately right in your position, you lose. The bank should have never argued with or shown suspicion of Mrs. Dewey.
- **Lesson Two.** Give customers a chance to teach you what they know about their position. Sometimes their lesson will point to their own errors—the process of discovery. If not, it may point toward your education. If the customer does prove to be your mentor, reward her with your allegiance. The bank could have learned much from Mrs. Dewey and found a way to affirm her contribution to the bank's continued financial success.
- **Lesson Three.** Never try to stop a runaway train with your bare hands. If a customer's anger moves from upset to livid, get out of the way and let the energy of the frontal assault wind down before attempting any sort of intervention. You can hasten the venting process through dramatic listening, lavish understanding, and absolutely

zero defensiveness. The bank should have given Mrs. Dewey a chance to vent and then channeled her energy into problem resolution, corrective action, and preventive maintenance.

- **Lesson Four.** If you are ever wrong (and you will be sometime), work harder to regain the customers' trust than you did to get their business. The only way to remove the residual of aggrievement is through a lot of attention and assuaging of bruised feelings. The bank, or at least her local branch, should have paid very close attention to Mrs. Dewey's monthly statements after the first mistake and followed up to rebuild her confidence. It would have only taken a few minutes.

The next sections are about making the most of those precious second chances customers give you for redemption and retention after service or product breakdowns.

Part Two

The Service Recovery Process

Eighty percent of customers' problems are caused by bad systems, not by bad people.

—John Goodman
President, TARP, Inc.

We marvel at the magician's craft. One—two—three—shazaam! A disappearing tiger. A levitating lady. A bullet caught in the teeth. We know, intellectually, that it is all illusion and artifice. But we marvel nonetheless. Great service recovery looks and feels like magic. And just as the memorable magician's artistry is no accident, organizations that excel at recovery have long ago mastered the art of making the impossible seem easy. First, they master their *method*. The root of the act must be rehearsed repeatedly. Practice not only makes perfect, it allows the practitioner to focus on more than fundamental performance. Mastery starts with a commitment to drill and rehearsal to bring the act to life and meld with personal style.

Recovery magicians also master their *medium*. The making of magic includes management of the energy field between the magician and the audience. Lights, sounds, pace, timing, and even smell combine to ensure the aura of awe. Mastery involves managing the entire network that connects product and service with patron.

Finally, great recovery magicians master their *market*. They not only respect their audience, they spend focused effort divining what spectators expect and what makes them swoon. And they never stop learning, because they know today's "oh, wow" will be tomorrow's "ho hum." Mastery for the magician includes knowing how the audience assesses enchantment.

When recovery is unplanned and haphazard, it looks like panic and sounds unprofessional. When it is planned and practiced, it looks and feels genuine and rich.

5

Service Recovery:

The Process

Some people probably think I'm crazy to go to all the trouble I do sometimes, but I just think of the patient. What if that was my grandmother? I'd stand on my head and drink water if it would help.

—Toni Omaits
SmithKline Beecham

First and foremost, service recovery is a set of actions that employees take to solve a customer problem and keep the customer from starting to think about a defection to the competition. Service recovery is about redress and retention. It is making sure that the original promise to the customer is kept—the customer gets what he or she came to you for—and restoring trust and confidence in your ability to make the customer whole.

Based on our and others' research into recovery behaviors and attitudes that customers expect and find memorable, we have developed a six-step process for handling the spectrum of unhappy customers, from the mildly disappointed to the toxically ticked-off (Figure 5-1). Applied consistently by customer-contact people, it has, in many controlled applications, led to an average twelve-point improvement in customer ratings of an organization's problem-solving ability.

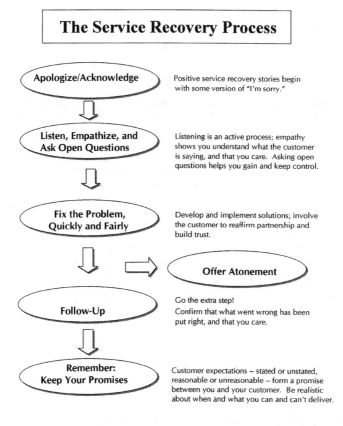

Figure 5-1. The service recovery process.

Step 1: Acknowledge that the customer has been inconvenienced and apologize for it.

It is critical that you apologize without condition, with no hint of defensiveness or shifting the blame to the customer. This is a key expectation and an important first step toward keeping a customer who feels aggrieved. Although a simple apology costs nothing to deliver, we find it forthcoming in fewer than 48

> **TIP: Apologize without accepting blame:**
>
> "I'd be unhappy if that happened to me."
>
> We have found that customer satisfaction increases 10 to 15 percent when the apology sounds genuine. By the way, apologizing for the customer's inconvenience does not imply that you are accepting fiduciary responsibility for the problem the customer is concerned about.

percent of the cases where a customer reports to a company that a problem exists with a product or service.

Apology is most powerful when delivered in the first person singular. The corporate "we're sorry" form letter lacks the sincerity and authenticity that comes with a personal, verbal acknowledgment delivered on behalf of the organization. A sincere, nonrobotic-sounding "I'm sorry for any inconvenience this late arrival may have caused you" suggests that the pilot, the lead flight attendant, or whoever is apologizing is taking a personal, professional interest in the situation. And, contrary to some fears, apologizing for the customer's inconvenience is not, and cannot be, interpreted as an admission of guilt or acceptance of legal culpability or liability. There is, in fact, some evidence that a simple apology alone can defuse a situation and prevent damaging escalation.

Step 2: Listen, empathize, and ask open-ended questions.

There is a clear and important difference between empathy (acknowledging and understanding the customer's emotional upset) and sympathy (sharing in the customer's anger with the organization and engaging in a mutual "misery fest"). Customers do not want service professionals to join them in "those guys in shipping should be shot" tirades. Rather, customers are looking for a good listener who allows them to explain their point of view and vent their frustrations, who shows an understanding of their upset, and who, by hearing them out, offers tacit evidence of believing the customers' report of the incident or error. A homily we first encountered at Digital Equipment Corporation (DEC), "The upset customer doesn't care how much you know, until he knows how much you care," is exceptionally wise when it comes to recovery.

Step 3: Offer a fair fix to the problem.

After the service provider acknowledges and addresses the emotional side of the service breakdown, he or she must correct the customer's problem. It is important the customer perceives the service provider as knowledgeable, empowered, and focused on a timely resolution. Contrary to common belief, customers typically bring a sense of fair play to the table when a situation calls for recompense or compensation. If the service provider offers a rational explanation and demonstrates sensitivity and concern, the customer usually responds in kind.

Asking customers what a fair fix for the problem might be often is quite revealing. When we asked telephone subscribers of an east coast telco what they expected from the company when service failures occurred, we found they clearly distinguished between a service failure that happened on a weekend and one that happened on a weekday, as well as between one that was the company's fault and one caused by an act of nature. They told us, in effect, that it was okay for the phone company to be more sluggish in its response on a midsummer weekend because, after all, "Sunday is a weekend, and most of them like to be home with their families just like we do." Their view of a "fair fix" was, it seems, highly situational.

Providing a full explanation of what happened and what will happen to fix the problem is critical. TARP has found employees' inability to explain reasons for a breakdown to be the most prevalent customer frustration in recovery efforts and the most easily fixed through training.

Customer expectations of recovery need careful study before an organization embarks on a systematic service recovery effort. Recovery expectations can vary by locale, customer demographics, and the recovery processes in place in other organizations that serve the customer in the same marketplace. If a large percentage of your customers also are customers of service exemplars such as Nordstrom or Federal Express, their experiences with those organizations will color their expectations and evaluation of you and your recovery efforts.

In most instances of recovery, these three steps suffice to fix your customer's problem and patch up the relationship. Approximately 70 percent of service recovery incidents require no gesture of atonement (step 4) and only a minimal of follow-up (step 6).

Step 4: Offer some value-added atonement for the inconvenience/injury.

We also call this step "symbolic atonement." Symbolic atonement is the free-dessert, complimentary home-delivery discount coupon and the partial or full refund offer that compensates the customer for the inconvenience or distress.

At the most basic level, atonement is a gesture that clearly says, "We want to apologize to you for your inconvenience." Atonement is more than simply the "It's on us," "Free drink," "No charge" offer. It is a demonstration of goodwill. The word "symbolic" is carefully chosen. It suggests that little things, when sincerely done, mean a lot to the customer. Customers do not expect us to offer to shoot the branch manager or provide a free trip to Walt Disney World for keeping them waiting in the reception area an extra 10 minutes. They *do* expect us to make a reasonable, small gesture that acknowledges the inconvenience.

There is an easy way to test our premise that customers have reasonable and modest recovery expectations. Create ten to twenty typical service breakdown scenarios, each ending with the question, "What do we need to do to make things right for this customer and win back his or her loyalty?" Then give the scenarios to ten customers in a focus group and to ten customer service representatives. Our experience is that, in the majority of cases, what customers ask for by way of atonement costs less and is easier to deliver than what your service representatives suggest. Customers prove to us over and over again that they hold imminently reasonable expectations of recovery in general and of atonement in particular.

NOTE: Atonement is not a requirement for successful recovery from every service or product breakdown. Rather, atonement is critical to satisfaction when the customer feels "injured" by the service delivery breakdown, when the customer feels victimized, greatly inconvenienced, or somehow damaged by the problem.

Sometimes, however, a custom-tailored or highly aggressive act of atonement might be necessary to keep a highly valued or long-time customer. And

sometimes a determined, proactive effort can both impress the customer and give your organization's reputation a nice boost. When management at L.L. Bean, the catalog retailer in Freeport, Maine, learned that a sport shirt it was selling had a tendency to fray at the collar after only a few washings, they took the initiative. Customers who had purchased the shirt received a letter, regardless of whether they had experienced fraying or not, informing them of the problem and encouraging return of the shirt. The letter further instructed that if returning the shirt was inconvenient, the Bean customer service unit would be pleased to arrange a pickup for the customer, a gesture that further emphasized the sincerity of Bean's offer.

When a customer of Buckner Inc., a Fresno, California-based irrigation products company, sent back for repair a couple of the company's brass sprinkler heads, employees did not think much of it. They would do the standard repair or simply send out new sprinklers as replacements. That was until they discovered the sprinklers were antique models, manufactured in 1948.

Buckner no longer makes sprinklers the same way—with leather washers—and did not have the parts needed for repair. But the customer had grown attached over the years to the hardware and did not want the offered replacements. According to the *Fresno Bee*, the sprinkler heads had been in the customer's family for three generations.

So Tony Garcia, a Buckner employee, took the sprinkler heads home over the weekend. There he fashioned some new leather washers from an old pair of shoes and sent the vintage sprinklers back, without charge. The customer, delighted beyond words, insisted on learning who had done the work. When told Garcia's name, the customer sent him a check for $25 to cover his labor. Equally important, the customer told the *Fresno Bee*, who told us, and we are telling you. The end result is a priceless polishing of Buckner's reputation. NOTE: When and how to offer atonement is one of the hardest things for front-line customer service people to learn. The best approach we have found is to draft a series of recovery cases, preferably real ones from your files, and a series of short (1- to 3-hour) training meetings to discuss the cases. Let your people propose solutions to the scenarios and, rather than present school answers, i.e., the "right" answers, discuss the pros and cons of the proposed palliatives.

Step 5: Keep your promises.

Customers sometimes are skeptical of a company's recovery promises. Their tendency is to believe that service representatives' promises aim primarily at getting the customer off the phone or out of the office, rather than actually solving the problem or fixing the customer's upset. Although bad news can prompt the customer to huff and bluster at the customer-contact employee, customers would rather hear straight talk or bad news than be told lies or misleading information. For example, customers would rather be informed that their flight may be up to 90 minutes late than be told of a 15-minute delay six different times. Somehow it is easier to endure a wait on hold, or sitting in a hot, cramped, delayed airliner, if you have been apprised of the real problem and its projected fix time.

Customers value, and happily share with others, the feats of customer service representatives who display a "can do" attitude

and ability. On the other hand, they frequently tell horror stories of promises made but broken, often for years after the incident.

Step 6: Follow-up.

Customers also are favorably impressed when a sales or customer service person follows up with them after the initial service recovery episode, usually via phone call, to make sure the solution is still satisfactory.

This after-the-fact service recovery satisfaction assessment is particularly important in breakdown situations where customers perceive that they may be "at risk" if they voice anger or are upset. For example, research conducted by Philip A. Newbold and Diane Stove r of Memorial Hospital in South Bend, Indiana, found that "because of fear of retaliation, some patients kept quiet (about service disappointments) until after discharge, particularly regarding nursing issues."[1] Following up gives the organization a second chance to solve the customer's problem if the first effort falls short of the customer's expectations, especially if the customer was reluctant to voice the complaint to you a second time.

Several years ago, one of us was on a follow-up call with a bank officer about a client whose payroll had been badly mangled two out of the last four payroll periods. The call was to assure that the problems now were sorted out to the client's satisfaction. "Now that we've had two error-free payroll periods, is everything okay? Are we back on an even keel?" the banker queried. To which the client retorted, "Heck no. I haven't had any reasonable grovel yet?" "Grovel?" "I'm the managing partner here. I need to be able to prove that this is fixed and you've been properly called on it," he explained. "How do we do that?" our companion asked. "I need a letter from the president of your bank admitting the problem was all on your end, that it's fixed, and that it can't happen again," the client advised. A small price

1. Philip Newbold and Diane Serbin Stover, *Health Care Forum Journal,* December 1994.

to pay. And a residual bad feeling we would never have uncovered without the follow-up call.

Follow-Up: The Second Meaning

Follow-up means following up with the customer, but it also means following up with the organization as well. Service representatives should be able to communicate easily inside their organizations to ensure that the solutions they put in motion actually are executed (the package was shipped, the account credited) and to allow recurring problems to be tracked, studied, and removed from the delivery system. Without internal follow-up, service recovery is a one-shot, spray-and-pray activity, not part of a planned, systematic effort to track and reduce service-related problems.

6

The Axioms of Elegant Service Recovery

The secret is to understand the customer's problems and provide solutions so as to help that customer be profitable and feel good about the transaction.

—Francis (Buck) Rodgers
Retired IBM sales guru

Axioms are the self-evident truths that underlie a course of action, a process, or a philosophy. All three are true of the axioms of service recovery. These five axioms are the research-based, customer-centered ideas and ideals that form the philosophy and principles on which the six-step recovery—actually the entire process of recovery—is based.

"Why," you might ask, "bother with a bunch of axioms? If the process works—it works." Good question. Forget the axioms. You can, sort of. The six-step process is a good one. But it is more powerful and certainly more flexible in the way front liners apply it when you, and they, have a solid grasp on these underlying core concepts.

Axiom 1: Customers Have Recovery Expectations

Expectations are the building blocks of all customer transactions, the embodiment of all the customer's wants and needs.

A customer's expectations can be as unique as the body shape and inner functioning of a doctor's patient. But, just as in medicine, there are fundamental similarities that can guide our efforts. The basic alikeness of two different human's kidneys enables physicians to perform kidney surgery using a reliable set of norms, protocols, and prognoses. There is an apt parallel in service—and service recovery—expectations. We all want personalized treatment, but our individual visions of what that entails can share a lot of similarities.

These expectations fall into five categories that, according to research by Berry, Zeithaml, and Parasuraman, cover 80 percent of the differences between high and low customer satisfaction scores.[1] These factors are as follows.

Reliability

Reliability encompasses all the actions that telegraph organizational competence. First and foremost, it means keeping promises or doing what you say you will do. We exude reliability when things work as they are supposed to or the way we say they will. Reliability is the backbone of dependability and faith. Reliability is the most critical of the five attributes of customer service and the key to understanding upset and ire when things go amiss. Why?

Most of us relish a high degree of predictability. We are comforted that the sun comes up every morning . . . and not on a random basis. When things do not happen as we predict or as we are told they will happen, it leaves us with high anxiety and a desire to put things back in balance. Breaking mutual agreements shatters any semblance of trust.

Assurance

Assurance is about confidence. It signals that things are going as they should. The doctor acts just like a doctor is supposed

1. Leonard Berry, Valarie Zeithaml, and A. Parasuraman, "Five Imperatives for Improving Service Quality," *Sloan Management Review*, Summer 1990: 29–38.

to act. The clerk acts knowledgeable, the pilot sounds self-assured, and the wine steward has a French accent (we made that last one up, but you get the point). Assurance is an array of emotional cues that tell the customer to "be assured, all is well, and everything in its place." When service breakdown occurs, assurance has a deeper, more poignant meaning.

Assurance is an unspoken guarantee or pledge. We often enter a service transaction with specific notions about what it ought to be like. We know our place, our lines, and our role. If, for reasons beyond our control, the service provider refuses to participate in the fashion expected, we feel out of control and in need of reassurance. A heavy dose of authenticity, coupled with a generous helping of confidence-building actions, is required in the recipe to quickly right the scene and honor the pledge. In service recovery, assurance is really reassurance that everything is okay or soon will be made so.

Tangibles

Tangibles are the physical "stuff" that goes with the service experience. By "goes with" we mean where its presence is appropriate and its absence an alarm. When the plumber shows up with dirt under his nails, we assume he has been busy and we are ready to open our basement doors. But if the dentist shows up in the same unkempt fashion, we assume he has lost his allegiance to hygiene and we are reluctant to open our mouths. Tangibles work in support of the other four attributes. Flowers make empathy more poignant; spit and polish make assurance more credible; and clean, accurate paperwork tells us we are working with precise professionals.

Although tangibles may not lead the list of culprits that turn customer content to contempt, they amplify our upset or unease, and they underscore our perception that the server's ambition is to disappoint us. When the hotel leaves cigarette butts in the ashtrays or the auto repair shop leaves grease on our windshield, we are insulted by their disrespect for our association and insulted by their disregard for our assets.

Empathy

Empathy includes all the actions you take to declare to customers that you genuinely care. Active listening, for instance, makes customers feel valued. Communicating regularly tells customers that you are attentive. We show empathy when we respond to customers' specific needs, when we keep them informed of important changes, and when we act in ways the customers deems fair, compassionate, honest, and thoughtful.

Empathy means understanding. And to understand at an emotional level requires a passionate *connection*. When trust has been challenged or threatened, the bridge to recovery starts with the most fundamental component of being human . . . a pure, genuine, and considerate link. It means someone in your organization must obviously and without reserve reach out to the customer when things go wrong.

NOTE: There is a difference between empathy and sympathy. *Sympathy* involves identifying with, and even taking on, another person's emotions. A sympathetic response is, "I'm really angry about those centerpieces, too." *Empathy* means acknowledging

TIP: When a service provider wallows in a customer's misfortune, there are two victims instead of one. As a service professional, you need to see the clear difference between what happened and who it happened to—and work on the former to bring things back to normal.

and affirming another's emotional state. An empathetic response is, "I can understand how that makes you angry."

The task is to be emotionally aware and sensitive without becoming too emotionally involved. When your customer service representatives (CSRs) respond with empathy, they stay calm and in control. Only then are they at their absolute best: ready, willing, and able to help the customer.

Showing empathy for customers actually allows the customer service representatives to be professional and caring at the same time. It also makes customers feel like important individuals. Empathy cannot be handed out by a machine; it is something one person does for another. There is no substitute for the human touch.

Responsiveness

Responsiveness is doing things in an appropriately timely fashion. It means the service provider's actions happen fast enough for the customer not to feel neglected but do not occur in a panicky way. It is more than the pace of service; it is also the perception of that pace. The auto repair shop that takes 2 hours to get a needed part gets lower marks than the one that takes the same 2 hours but keeps the customer posted on where the part is and when it is expected. We Homo sapiens hate to be kept in the dark. Questions and answers are a fundamental ingram—building block—of interpersonal communication. Without communication, we feel isolated, alone, and powerless in the face of a service breakdown.

The dark side of responsiveness is not nonresponsiveness, it is indifference. We interpret the truancy of reply (i.e., the faltering of action) as a calculated and callused affront to our need for an answer. We are left angered by its absence—and doubly angered by our dependence on it. Our deep-seated reaction suggests that communication be rapid and regular after service breakdowns, and that responses prove sufficiently abundant to rebuild our reserve.

Axiom 2: Successful Recovery Is Psychological as Well as Physical: Fix the Person, Then the Problem

Customers who have a problem with your product or service expect you to solve the problem. Just as important, but less easy for customers to articulate, is the need to be "fixed" psychologically. Often a customer who has a bad experience with your company or product loses faith in your reliability—your ability to deliver what you promised. The repair person who goes straight to the copier or laser printer, completes the repair task, and quietly leaves for the next call may be practicing good technical work-unit-per-hour management, but not good recovery. The customer-contact person who needed to use the broken machine and was under pressure to get it fixed needs to be "repaired" as well. If nothing more, the service person needs to give the contact person an opportunity to vent his or her pent-up frustration. It is part of the job.

The core of the psychological aspect of recovery is restoring trust—the customer's belief that you can and will keep both the explicit and implicit promises you make. Trust is particularly at risk when the customer feels vulnerable, that is, perceives all the power to set things right is in your hands, and little or nothing is under his or her control. That sense of vulnerability—and the customer's reaction to the breakdown—is the loudest when the customer feels he or she lacks:

Information: They do not know what is going on or how long it will take to set things right.

Expertise: The customer could not fix the car or computer or fouled-up reservation on a bet. All the "smarts" are on your side of the table.

Freedom: There is no option for fixing the problem aside from dealing with you. The customer perceives you as his or her only hope.

Recourse: The customer perceives that when it comes to this computer or car or malady, it is you or nobody. They may be free, contractually, to ask anyone else they can find to do the problem "fix," but there is no one else, or at least they see it that way.

Restoring trust is accomplished by involving the customer in solving the problem, "Tell me again exactly what was happening when it stopped," or "Can you give me a run-down on the history of this problem," and reassuring the client that the problem is fixable and will be.

Process wise, it is critical to fix—deal with and reassure—the customer before plunging into fixing the problem. The most important "customer fixing" skill your people can develop is listening. Letting the customer tell his or her tale, blow off steam, and give you his or her point of view—plus a sincere apology from you—goes a long way toward the needed psychological fix.

Axiom 3: Work in a Spirit of Partnership

Our research suggests strongly that customers who participate in the problem-solving effort are more satisfied with the problem resolution. There are, however, limits and provisos to this dictum. When the company clearly causes the problem, asking the customer what he or she would like to see happen next gives the customer a sense of regaining control. That regained sense of control can be vital to calming customers who feel that the organization treated them unjustly or in some way abused them or who are bordering on a perception that they were victimized or treated unfairly.

When the customer clearly caused the problem, asking him or her to do something to help facilitate solving the problem is appropriate and increases the probability that the customer will feel satisfied with the solution. The solution, in both situations, becomes our solution, not your solution.

Critical to creating a sense of partnership is the way you invite the customer into the problem-solving process. The query, "So, what do you want me to do about it?," may be seen as shifting the responsibility for managing the service recovery process back onto the customer.

Remember those old movies when the doctors send the father off to "boil water" in preparation for a home birth? By and large, the water boiling assignment was a way of keeping the father out of the way, occupied and feeling a part of the process. Even if all the customer can really do, metaphorically, is boil water, the effort has palliative effects.

The bank customer who failed to endorse her paycheck when she deposited it and thereby caused a string of bounced checks feels better about the recovery effort when she is given a part in the redress. An assignment such as "Give me a list of all the people you've written checks to" or "call the people you've written checks to and ask them to resubmit them for payment" gives the customer back some sense of psychological control.

Axiom 4: Customers React More Strongly to "Fairness" Failures Than to "Honest Mistakes"

Researcher Kathleen Seiders from Babson College, Wellesley, Massachusetts, found that "When customers believe they have been treated unfairly, their reactions tend to be immediate, emotional and enduring."[2] In other words, if the customer feels he or she has been short changed, given short shrift, or disrespected on purpose, the reaction is heated and long lasting.

There is but one course of action when the customer feels treated unfairly: extreme apology and atonement. Sure, the customer's prescription may indeed be the result of a misunderstanding of something said or done and not intended. That is ir-

---

2. Kathleen Seiders and Leonard Berry, "Service Fairness: What It Is and Why It Matters," *Academy of Management Executive*, 12(2)1990: 8–20.

What Focus Group Members Remembered and Found Impressive	Interviewees Who Commented On and Were Impressed by This Action
• CSR dealt with my upset	79.0%
• CSR apologized	69.1%
• CSR did not become defensive, but showed humility and poise	62.9%
• CSR followed up after the complaint transaction	56.8%
• CSR showed skill at problem solving	53.0%
• CSR, when appropriate, was proactive in admitting organization error, did not try to shift blame	44.4%
• CSR acted in a fully responsible and empowered fashion on the customer's behalf	40.7%
• CSR showed good interpersonal skills, particularly listening	40.7%
• CSR showed empathy for the customer's plight and/or upset	38.3%
• CSR acted quickly to solve the problem, showed urgency	35.8%
• CSR created added value for the customer	32.1%
• CSR believed the customer, valued the customer's perception	24.7%

Note: Performance Research Associates conducted eighty-one focus group and discussion sessions. They asked customers what they expected and what they had experienced as positive from companies when they experienced a service breakdown. The average group size was twelve discussants, with individual groups ranging from eight to twenty participants.

relevant. Once a customer feels unfairly treated, you are dealing with an at-risk customer and, according to Seiders, a customer who is a prime candidate for overt, hostile, retaliation. Seiders suggests communication (explaining what went wrong) and compensation (atonement) can repair a perception of unfairness.

It is important, she adds, to cast the explanation in terms that do not attempt to put the full responsibility for the faux pas on the shoulders of a third party or a "misunderstanding." The direct, simple, "I'm sorry this has occurred and I'll make sure it is cleared up right away" is as close to a magic bullet as there is in service recovery.

Axiom 5: Effective Recovery Is a Planned Process

Airlines and hotels overbook. Trains and planes have weather delays and cancellations. If uncontrollable conditions can cause problems for your customers, creating a planned process makes imminent sense. However, you must institute and apply the planned process in a highly responsive, customer-sensitive fashion. Customers remember uncaring, robotic recovery long after they forget the incident that necessitated the solution.

It is important that front-line service employees know what you expect planned recovery to look like and where the

---

Top Ten Service Expectations of Bank Retail Customers

1. Being called back when promised
2. Receiving an explanation of how a problem happened
3. Knowing who to contact with a problem
4. Being contacted promptly when a problem is resolved
5. Being allowed to talk to someone in authority
6. Being told how long it will take to resolve a problem
7. Being given useful alternatives if a problem cannot be solved
8. Being treated like a person, not an account number
9. Being told about ways to prevent a future problem
10. Being given progress reports if a problem cannot be solved immediately

Note: Research conducted by Linda Cooper of Cooper and Associates, Evanston, Illinois.

limits to recovery lie. It is also critically important that they regularly practice implementing the plan. Customers remember two things from well-designed and well-implemented planned recovery: the quality of the solutions offered and the skill of the people offering it. Of the two, the latter is the most memorable.

Planned Recovery in Action

The lobby is deserted. It is not hard to overhear the conversation between the night manager at the Marriott Long Wharf Hotel in Boston and the late arriving guest.

"Yes, Dr. Jones, we've been expecting you. I know you are scheduled to be here three nights. I'm sorry to tell you, sir, but we are booked solid tonight. A large number of guests we assumed were checking out did not. Where is your meeting tomorrow, sir?"

The doctor told the clerk where it was.

"That's near the Omni Parker House! That's not very far from here. Let me call them and get you a room for the evening. I'll be right back."

A few minutes later the desk clerk returned with the good news.

"They're holding a room for you at the Omni Parker House, sir. And, of course, we'll pick up the tab. I'll forward any phone calls that come here for you. Here's a letter that will explain the situation and expedite your check-in, along with my business card so you can call me directly here at the front desk if you have any problems."

The doctor's mood was moving from exasperation toward calm. But the desk clerk was not finished with the encounter. He reached into the cash drawer. "Here are two $5 bills. That should more than cover your cab fare from here to the Parker House and back again in the morning. We don't have a problem tomorrow night, just tonight. And here's a coupon that will get you complimentary continental breakfast on our concierge level on the fifth floor tomorrow morning . . . and again, I am so sorry this happened."

As the doctor walks away, the night manager turns to the desk clerk, "Give him about 15 minutes and then call to make sure everything went okay."

A week later, the same guest who had overhead the exchange is in a taxi, en route to the same hotel. Along the way, he tells of the great service recovery episode he had witnessed the week before. The pair arrive at the hotel and make their way to the front desk—ready to check in.

There they are greeted with unexpected news:

"I am so sorry gentlemen. I know you were scheduled to be here for two nights. But we're booked solid tonight. Where is your meeting scheduled tomorrow?"

The would-be guests exchange a rueful glance as they give the desk clerk their future plans.

"That's near the Meridian. Let me call over there and see if I can get you a room. It won't take but a minute."

As the clerk walks away, the tale teller says, "I'll bet he comes back with a letter and a business card."

Sure enough, the desk clerk returns to deliver the solution; not a robotic script, but all the elements from the previous week's show were on display. What the tale teller thought he witnessed the previous week as pure desk-clerk initiative he now realizes was planned, a spontaneous-feeling yet predetermined response to a specific category of customer problem.

The point at which your customer is most insecure is where your organization's front line should be most confident. In other words, *at that juncture where your customer is most insecure because things are not turning out as anticipated, your front line should be best equipped to ease the anxiety.* Planned recovery arms front-line service people with the confidence and competence to turn distress into delight.

7

Recovery and the Internet/ E-Commerce

Wake up every morning terrified—not of your competition, but of your customers.

—Jeff Bezos
CEO, Amazon.com

No talk of service recovery is complete without mentioning the new game in town and the constellation of high-stakes service challenges it brings with it: e-commerce. More organizations are taking to the web to shop their wares, and figures show that growing numbers of us now prefer to shop with a mouse rather than at the mall. Analysts predict the percentage of business conducted online will grow exponentially in the next 5 years: 1999 holiday sales hit an estimated $12 billion, an approximate 300 percent increase from 1998 figures. Forrester Research projects that business-to-business commerce will grow from $43 billion in 1998 to $1 trillion in 2003.

But plenty of e-tailers still are focused only on acquiring customers, not servicing them, and thus are learning hard lessons when it comes to the ripple effects of poor customer care. Cobbling together a visually stunning consumer web site is one thing; creating the customer support, online problem help, ease of navigation, and other shopper-friendly features needed to keep e-shoppers coming back beyond one blood-boiling visit is quite another. More so than ever, when you move online, it is not what you sell, but how you sell it—the wraparound of the customer experience—that separates you from the masses of e-commerce and dot.com wannabees. And that raises the stakes higher for good service recovery online. Experts agree that the standard for customer support must be higher for the web than it is in the offline, face-to-face, and over-the-phone retail worlds.

The first few years of e-shopping have been rife with horror stories of refunds never credited to credit cards, inventory shortages, web sites crashes due to heavy traffic, unanswered e-mail, late product delivery or delivery to wrong addresses, and much more. And therein lies the scary part for management: Customers are proving there is nothing quite as easy as typing in a competitor's URL if they've had some frustrating, logic-refuting, or unresolved service problems at *www.Acme.com.* It makes face-to-face retail seem glacial and catalog customer abandonment tortoise-like. As Melinda Goddard of Roche says, "Word of mouse can have a much greater impact than word of mouth."

Managing customer expectations has proved to be a big bugaboo for e-sellers. Online shoppers start out with high expectations of the virtual shopping experience, fueled in part by the nature of the web itself. Customers who can shop around the clock now expect around-the-clock service, something they would never think of demanding from traditional brick-and-

mortar companies. When they visit web sites and send out
e-mail requests for help or more information, many expect a response within an hour or two, not realizing or caring that the service rep on the receiving end might have a few hundred other
queries to answer at the same time. In other cases, companies
themselves fan the flames of unrealistic expectations. Their aggressive advertising messages suggest that online shopping is a
breeze, and that customers will have little problem getting rapid
response to e-mail, contacting live phone reps with questions, receiving quick and reliable product delivery, or returning product purchased online, promises in many cases they are ill
equipped to deliver on.

As a result of these and other such problems, companies
moving whole-hog into e-commerce need to stand ready to deal
with a new strain of customer complaint: the "cybervent" or
complaint lodged via e-mail. More so even than phoning 800
contact numbers, unhappy customers find the detached distance
of e-mail a license to complain more regularly and often with
more emotional fervor. Need evidence? According to a report in
USA Today's Weekend version, in 1999 the National Consumers
League received up to 1,000 online filed complaints a month,
compared to just 600 per month in 1998. The Federal Trade Com-
mission received an average of 4,800 online complaints a month
in 1999, up from only 2,000 a month in 1998.

Without a strong online problem-resolution strategy, companies can find their call centers overrun when they unveil new
products on the web or when customers begin experiencing
problems with existing ones.

Other studies indicate that e-shoppers' service-related problems are not abating. Resource Marketing, a Columbus, Ohio-
based consulting group that critiques e-commerce sites, tested 45
consumer web sites in the summer of 1999 and found only 60
percent bothered to respond to customer e-mail inquiries at all.
Less than ten of those sites had prominent guarantees offering
full refunds to unsatisfied customers. And only one-third of
these e-tailers would accept returns of products purchased online at their brick-and-mortar stores. In another study, reported
in the *Minneapolis Star Tribune*, market research firm Jupiter
Communications sent e-mails requesting help to 125 top web

sites. Almost half (46 percent) either took 5 or more days to respond to the request, never responded, or did not post an e-mail address on the site. That number was up from 38 percent in 1998.

And the Boston Consulting Group found that traditional retailers and catalog companies currently spend nearly five times as much on customer service and retention as do online retailers.

The data add up to trouble for companies slow to build the infrastructure needed to help customers do more than just peruse products online. Customer loyalty on the web may be even more fleeting than when customers shop the traditional way, and companies that view customer service as nothing more than an afterthought are likely to pay a steep price by missing out on chances to capture a big piece of a mushrooming sales channel, to boost web site advertising revenues, and to ensure that Wall Street looks kindly on its future revenue and profit-building prospects.

Some do get it, of course. At Lands' End, the Wisconsin-based clothing retailer, if you have trouble finding what you want on their web site, you can simply click on a button, type in your phone number, and a salesperson will call you back within no time. The company also offers a "live chat box" to allow shoppers to talk to salespeople while checking out products online. The Gap and Amazon.com are others that routinely get high marks for customer support, personalized service, and reliable product delivery.

Preliminary Rules of the Road

Although e-commerce rules for success are yet developing, there are some emerging guidelines. Here are a few simple rules of the road to help you follow in the footsteps of those e-service exemplars, to make your web site more shopper friendly, to give customers ways to get nagging problems resolved or questions answered more quickly, and to ensure you are not driving away business in what likely will prove an increasingly valuable sales channel. These are gleaned from our own experience shopping web sites, from the input of our cybershopping colleagues, and from industry experts who evaluate web sites for a living.

- **Make sure customers can find a phone number.** Far too many consumer web sites do not list a phone number, or the number is difficult to locate. Post an 800 number prominently on your home page so it is easy for e-customers to find and follow up for live help if they need it.

  In theory, at least, a shift to more web-based service and online support should free up phone reps to deliver more in-depth help.
- **Create one-click help.** Help for customers , whether it involves product availability, billing, order confirmation, delivery tracking, or other oft-requested information, should never be more than one click away. You want customers to click because they are engaged, not desperately confused. Do not force them to click endlessly into a carpal tunnel seizure to find what they need. Web site designers still too often allow customers to land in dead-end spots where they cannot easily ask for more information or post e-mail requests.

- **Create a list of frequently asked questions.** Frequently asked questions (FAQs) take the pressure off live phone or online support by giving customers easy and around-the-clock access to the most commonly asked questions about your e-shopping outlet. Some experts advise creating two layers of FAQs: one for prospective or new customers with fundamental questions and another for continuing customers who are familiar with your products or services.

  Heavy use of FAQs can be an early warning system. If customers are accessing the service frequently, there might be problems with your advertising, marketing, product user manuals, packaging, or the like. It may be prudent to install a proactive recovery system in the vein of the Gracie Golf system as described in Chapter 2.

- **Create standards and training for e-mail response.** To help modulate customer expectations, set standards for response time to e-mail inquiries, then train your people how to use this new tool to answer questions and address problems in customer-sensitive ways.

  The web is an immediate medium, and long delays in response times can dull customer loyalty. Once a customer has been disappointed by how slowly questions are answered or problems resolved, they are not likely to try again.

  Lands' End receives about 400 such e-mail requests daily, and staffers have a standard of responding within 3 hours. At Dell Computer, support technicians answer most customer e-mails within 4 hours.

  In the spirit of keeping online customers apprised and updated, consider creating some form of "auto acknowledgment" that responds to customers' incoming e-mail requests, states that the question was received, and sends back a response estimating a time frame for how long it might take to answer the question.

- **Organize your site with the customer, not your web designers, in mind.** Simplicity and clarity, *not* artistic sophistication, are the watchwords for commercial web site design. It should be easy for customers to navigate your site, find whatever they need in a hurry, and understand the labeling and language once they arrive. Information-rich but poorly designed pages send customers scurrying back to the brick-and-mortar world in a hurry. And make sure your web site's search engines are up to the job; many generate too many results or cannot handle long queries.

Another issue is slow download times. Most web site designers use state-of-the-art equipment, so it is easy to forget that the majority of e-shoppers have less sophisticated computers, slow modems, and smaller monitors. Long download times resulting from heavy-handed or superfluous use of multimedia content, Java applets or dense screens, or other whiz-bang elements can destroy customers' desire to "stick with it" or return for another try.

- **Make sure your product return channels are synchronized and complement each other.** Customers are none too pleased when they order product from a web site, only to find they cannot return it at the company's brick-and-mortar version. Make sure your return policies are synchronized for easy in-person product return. If your accounting system can distinguish between e-commerce and face-to-face sales, it can learn to distinguish between the origins of returned merchandise.

- **Limit order form pain.** E-sites usually require customers to fill out lengthy forms before they can order product. Order forms are a necessary evil, but streamlining yours where possible can help put you a cut above the pack. A study by Jupiter Communications found that 27 percent of online buyers abandon at least one online order before completion because the order form is driving them up the wall. By contrast, Jupiter reports, only 19 percent of customers in its studies drop out because they were worried about online security.

- **Create your own e-service evaluation checklist.** When market research firms rate consumer web sites for service performance, they use criteria including product availability, order tracking, responsiveness to e-mail, personalization, giveaways, product return policies, postpurchase service, and quality of digital shopping carts. Consider building your own checklist to regularly critique how easy it is for e-customers to do business with you. Better yet, hire a dozen "civilians," citizen Internet shoppers to comparison-shop your site and the sites of both your competitors and a select set of world-class benchmark quality sites.

Part Three

Creating a Strategic Service Recovery System

Customers don't expect you to be perfect. They do expect you to fix things when they go wrong.

—Donald Porter
Senior Vice President, British Airways

At first blush, great service recovery looks like a lot of carefully selected and trained, highly motivated, unflappable superstar service people plucking victory from the jaws of defeat. Done well, distinctive service recovery looks like that: well-oiled magic, delivered by almost superhuman service pros. Done to distinction, it looks easy, natural, and effortless.

But beneath the line of visibility, under the water line, so to speak, is a well thought-out and carefully designed system that supports that flawless, smooth performance the customer sees. The core of that system is

- A set of rules, policies, and procedures that empower employees to fit the right solution to the right problem for the right customer
- A service quality improvement system that uses the opportunities presented by recovery incidents to squeeze error out of the service production process

It takes both, done well, to make service recovery a strategically important and operationally sound process and effort.

8

Creating a Service Recovery System

Eighty percent of customers' problems are caused by bad systems, not by bad people.

—John Goodman
TARP

We have alluded several times to the idea that service recovery is a *system* composed of multiple components, only one of which is the actual recovery transaction between the customer and a representative of your organization. For service recovery to be more than a process for cleaning up after slapdash service and products that perform poorly, it also must serve as a resource for systematic improvement of primary processes that create products and services. Berry and Parasuraman have identified three major outcomes of an effective service recovery system[1]:

- It identifies service problems.
- It resolves problems effectively.
- The organization learns from the recovery experience.

These three outcomes provide a robust framework. Figure 8-1 shows an adaptation based on the guidance provided by this framework. It details the Berry/Parasuraman framework as we interpret it. The goal is to suggest the activities and mechanisms

1. Leonard Berry and A. Parasuraman, *Marketing Services: Competing through Quality* (New York: The Free Press, 1991).

73

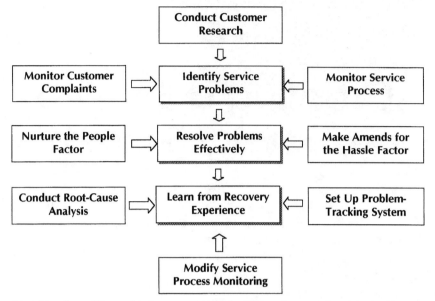

Adapted from Leonard Berry and A. Parasuraman, *Marketing Services: Competing through Quality* (New York: The Free Press, 1991).

Figure 8-1. Outcomes of an effective service recovery system.

an organization needs to put in place to maximize the service recovery effort.

Identifying Service Problems

The purposes of the process to identify problems are to capture historical and emerging information about organizational errors and problems that need to be corrected and expunged and to make sure that customers with problems are managed effectively. The three basic streams of this information are customer research, assessing customer complaints, and monitoring processes.

Customer Research

This is proactive customer (not market) research focused on customers with complaints about the organization's products or services. The search is for complaints not commonly reported and recovery expectations not previously understood. It is a search for the causes of customer acceptance, satisfaction, or disappointment with recovery and the causes. The keys to effective customer recovery research are to look for the unfound, the unusual, and the unexpected. Asking unusual questions helps, as does looking at and analyzing historical customer complaint and disappointment information in unusual ways. Also helpful is focusing on customer satisfaction and dissatisfaction with problem resolution. For example, one managed-care firm in the northwestern United States found that complaints to its member relations groups represented only 15 percent of actual customer complaints. The other 85 percent of complaints were voiced to doctors and clinic staff members who, overwhelmingly, did nothing with the information.

Effective tools for researching customer problems are focus groups, paper and pencil, telephone surveys, Internet surveys, customer intercepts, employee logs, and mystery shoppers.

Assessing Customer Complaints

It is important to examine incoming customer complaints in a timely fashion to spot emerging problem trends and newly developing delivery-system deficiencies. The complaint-handling system is also a vehicle for spotting and thinking through new situations that service reps need to respond to in the near future. Early warning, action planning, and planned follow-up opportunity are the keys to real-time customer complaint assessment.

Monitoring Processes

Monitoring the process of serving customers and of handling customer complaints is important for keeping the transaction quality clean, positive, and on track. The goal is to look for spots where the systems for serving customers and creating recovery are bent, if not broken. It is about finding real and potential fail points and repairing them. Good tools for the job are mystery shopping, simple observation, and creation of detailed service blueprints and maps.

Resolving Problems Effectively

Prepare People and Keep Them Fit

Good recovery depends on finding, training, and retaining good people. Good people are those with the strength to withstand the barbs of unhappy customers and with the learned cool to search for solutions to customer problems in the customer's presence.

Effective preparation of good people begins with hiring.

- Hire the right people.
- Screen technical people for customer skills.
- Train employees in the psychology of customers, problem solving, customer handling, and product knowledge.
- Empower employees to deal with customer problems and to resolve them on the spot. Give them the time and tools to do the job the way you want it done. Technology is essential.
- Reward and recognize excellent performance.

Create a Recovery Track and Solution Spaces

The focus of the recovery track is to help front-line service representatives heal broken customer relationships and keep customers. The process, such as our six-step process outlined in Chapter 5, emphasizes apology, listening, empathy skills, rapid resolution, added value, treatment, compensation, and, where useful, customer education.

Solution spaces provide a specific plank protocol or model to follow in specific service breakdown situations. For example, most airlines have a protocol for overbooked flights. The protocol tells employees exactly what types of compensation and alternative arrangements to make for bumped passengers. A good solution space matrix suggests atonement that is valuable and real. When airlines find enough volunteers to avoid bumping unwilling travelers, it is because their atonement offer (free tickets or travel vouchers) is a good balance for the inconvenience of taking a different, often later, flight.

For the solution to be effective in the eyes of the customer, the deliverer must not use it is as an excuse to treat the breakdown in a trivial or off-handed fashion. The apology for inconvenience, the problem correction, and the offer of compensation must be treated seriously.

Learning from Recovery Experience

An effective service recovery learning look sends information about product and service problems back into the product and service production system.

The methods described earlier feed data into tracking and root-cause analysis processes that create usable information for confirming or correcting the functioning of the product and service delivery production system.

This organizational learning component has several features:

- A problem-tracking system
- A root-cause analysis process
- Flexible service process monitoring

Interestingly, according to a TARP NASM study, only 11 percent of American companies have all three features.

Problem-Tracking System

The focus of a recovery tracking system is measurement of the customer retention and delivery improvement effort. It should answer two questions:

- Does the problem-resolution process actually result in customer satisfaction and retention?
- Does feeding product and service breakdown information back to the production cycle result in improved products and service delivery?

Keys to an effective problem-tracking system are contact tracking, assessment of problem resolution satisfaction, and problem-trend analysis.

It also is important that feedback from the recovery system to product and service production be "decriminalized," that is, information from the recovery system must be seen as valuable and valued.

Root-Cause Analysis Process

Whether housed within the service recovery function or within the system that creates services and products, information from the recovery process should feed into a root-cause analysis process. To create acceptance of the information that goes from the recovery function to a production function, a joint-problem analysis process is preferable.

Keys to an effective root-cause analysis system are training in analytical techniques, time available for data analysis, and permission to make process improvement suggestions.

Flexible Service Process Monitoring

A good service recovery system frequently uncovers service delivery fail points that heretofore were unidentified and thus unmonitored. The service recovery function, therefore, must have the flexibility and permission to establish monitoring or feedback systems of these previously unmonitored fail points.

Keys to monitoring service processes are the skills to establish such systems within the recovery system and the permission to create new monitoring efforts as need is perceived.

The People Side of Recovery Systems

A level down from the recovery system diagrammed and explained earlier is an operational system that deals with policies and procedures, people and problems. The specifics of that operating system can depend on an almost infinite number of variables. Your industry, your market niche, your market position, the labor market, and the economy are but a few. Regardless of the variations reality imposes on its design, we have found that there are five basic factors of varying degree of tangibility that accrue to recovery systems whose efforts are applauded by customers.[2]

2. These five factors are derived from the Services Management Practices Inventory (SMPI™), a 70,000-case survey database proprietary to Performance Research Associates and Questar Data Systems, Eagen, Minnesota.

1. **Employees are trained in the fine points of handling customer problems, know the common kinds of problems encountered by customers, and are skilled at enlisting the customer in generating acceptable solutions.** Implied in this factor is personal flexibility and organizational empowerment.

2. **Formal standards and informal norms reinforce the message to solve customer problems quickly and with a minimum of inconvenience for the customer and encourage an attitude of going "above and beyond" for the customer.** Important to this factor is the clear, unequivocal, and often voiced expectation that "above and beyond" for aggrieved customers is not only allowed, but it is encouraged.

3. **Systems, policies, and procedures focus on making it easy for customers to report problems or to complain and for employees to respond.** Customers who know that voicing concerns is important to the organization and see a mechanism for those reports in place are much easier for customer service representatives to work with. Front lines tell the difference.

4. **Front-line employees are confident problems will stay solved and that others in the organization will work as hard on the customer's problem as they themselves.** Employees who see themselves as the only people in the organization who are concerned about helping customers with problems—or interested in keeping those problems from occurring—soon lose interest in going to bat for customers as well. It seems a lose-lose proposition to them. When they receive support from other parts of the organization, they take their responsibility seriously.

5. **Front-line employees are confident that everyone is as concerned about recovery and customer satisfaction as they are.** Line employees watch to see how much effort other employees put into solving customer problems and customer satisfaction. They particularly watch the management team and judge how well and how often they "walk the talk."

9

Creating Consistent Solutions:

The Solution Space Approach

When your customer is the most anxious, you need to be at your best—competent, confident, calm, and in control of yourself.

—Chip R. Bell
Performance Research Associates

The first goal of service recovery is to create a sense of personalized response. Breakdowns and errors are taken very personally, and the expectation is that the redress will be as personal as the insult. The customer requires, and more correctly just assumes, the service provider has the capacity to create a tailored solution. At the same time, the organization requires some measure of rationality and responsibility. The balance is critical. We all know how to thrill an aggrieved customer. Give them whatever they want and more. However, such reckless responsiveness can bankrupt an organization or, at the least, dispirit service employees. The organization has a crucial stake in the recovery game. Although generosity typically is lauded in the quest for customer loyalty, too much abundance over time leaves the corporate coffers empty.

You own an automobile dealership. You want to be renowned for great service delivered by empowered employees. It is a late Friday afternoon in mid-July, and you are away at a meeting on the other side of town. The temperature is a sweltering 90 degrees. A customer shows up, family in tow, complaining that the air conditioning on his week-old car is defective. Your technicians check it out and confirm the customer's diagnosis. It will take 8 hours to repair; the car can be ready Monday after 4 P.M. The customer requests a loaner.

What decision do you want your employee to make?

On its surface, the choice might seem a no-brainer: Give the customer a loaner. But a few additional facts. Your on-site decision maker knows this customer has shopped a 2-hour radius of your dealership and only bought this car from you because you were the least expensive. The dealership made just $100 on the sale. The only repair work you are likely to get is major warranty work, like this air conditioner problem. Do you still want your people to respond the same way?

Let us up the price of playing the game. The reason this customer wants a loaner is to take his family on a camping trip—to the north woods! They were all set to leave on vacation when the air conditioner broke down. He will need the loaner for 2 weeks.

Now, what decision do you want your employee to make?

Hold on—we are not through yet. This is not the only automobile this customer has caused to be purchased from you. He happens to be the purchasing manager for a major corporation in a nearby town. Last year he directed his company to buy fifty new autos from you. Any change in the decision you want your employee to make?

Recovery decision making becomes more complicated when extenuating circumstances—reality—creeps into the picture. Yet the last thing you want are employees who have to run to you every time the decision making gets dicey. How do you equip front-line employees with decision-making skills that combine smart guidance with responsible freedom?

Solution Spaces: A Montessori Approach to Recovery

Maria Montessori was a gifted French educator whose work formed the basis for Montessori schools throughout the world. At the core of her philosophy is "creativity through structure." The approach directs teachers to add structure to the "mindless" part of a child's learning environment—where the blocks go, the child's place in the story circle, the layout of accessories when preparing to color—which frees the child to funnel energy into higher-level thinking.

That concept is one of the bases for the idea of service recovery "Solution Spaces."[1] A Solution Space provides a framework for decision making, offering clear guidance near the edges and space for latitude and creativity in the middle. In the case of the auto dealership, it would be like telling your customer service people, "Loaners are available *when* you think it is appropriate,

1. The term "solution space" technically comes from higher mathematics. In higher math, few problems have exacting answers. More correctly, their answers are contained in a solution space or set of bounded parameters. An infinite number of solutions can be correct, as long as they are contained in the solution space created by the defined parameters. By analogy, there is no perfect single answer to most recovery situations. There are too many variables and unique situations. But there is a bounded space where a number of good answers reside—a Solution Space.

for the *length of time* you think it appropriate, but that time should not exceed 2 days for customers who are first-time buyers, a week for repeat buyers, and a month for anyone on our 'diamond' customer list." Of course, trying to remember half a dozen pages of this sort of prose guideline is probably much too complex for normal human consumption, and the likely lists of explanatory and qualifying provisions would only confuse matters more. But boiling that long-winded guidance into a decision-making framework and talking through examples make for a manageable, learnable "Solution Space." Like this:

---

1. Is the customer's car problem of our making?   ❏Yes ❏No
2. Does the problem put the customer in need of a special or unusual accommodation?   ❏Yes ❏No
3. Is the customer a long-time or unusually important customer?   ❏Yes ❏No

If the answer to all three questions is YES, do whatever you can to accommodate the customer.

Let's look at the Solution Space idea applied to another recovery decision. A customer walks into a crowded fast-food restaurant at noon to order a sandwich, soft drink, and small order of french fries to go. On reaching the front of the line and placing his order, he is informed that it will be a short wait for his sandwich.

When the sixth customer behind him receives her order before he receives his, the customer's patience begins to run out, and it is obvious to everyone in the vicinity. Finally, the cashier presents the customer with his order, "I'm so very sorry this took so long," she says, "and I realize you were in a big hurry. Because you had to wait like this, I gave you a large order of fries at no extra charge. I hope you will come back and give us another chance." The customer's upset dissolves into a meek, "Oh, that's all right."

Where did this front liner develop the savvy to spot—and meet—this recovery need? What gave her the confidence and authority to make a judgment that favored the customer, but also put the register receipts out of balance with the raw potato inventory? Wasn't her manager concerned about excesses? Today she gave away extra fries; might she give away a trunkload of sandwiches tomorrow?

The reality is this restaurant's front-line employee knew in advance exactly how to respond to this particular customer problem. She had been trained in applying this "Solution Space" for a host of service breakdown scenarios. She had been given clear boundaries for a set of predictable circumstances, but with enough latitude to allow creativity and flexibility in a "Don't Fight, Make it Right!" recovery approach. In this specific case, the fast-food worker had been taught that:

- If the customer is upset...

- And, it's our fault in the eyes of the customer...

Then you can upgrade the customer's fries, upgrade his/her drink order, give him/her a free order of hash browns, or offer him/her a free dessert.

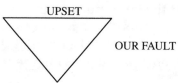

As long as your solution falls within the space, you decide what's needed to restore the customer's satisfaction with our products or service.

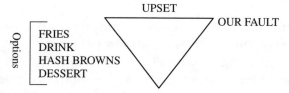

The "best" Solution Spaces give guidance but leave room (where appropriate) for choice and even a little creativity. And the guidance the Solution Space delivers should be general enough to cover a variety of situations, but without being so general as to invite wild excess. Imbedded examples help set the right tone.

Here are two examples of that design that come from banking.

Figure 9-1 is a Solution Space designed to give guidance in a situation where the problem was caused by something the *organization* did or failed to do for, or on behalf of, a customer. The Solution Space explains the goal the customer service representative (CSR) should have in mind and gives an example of the kind of actions that have been effective in the past.

The Solution Space in Figure 9-2 is for a problem that resulted from something the *customer* did, or failed to do, that needs the bank's help to fix.

Key to the difference between the Figure 9-1 and Figure 9-2 solution spaces is that the latter puts some of the responsibility for fair fixing the problem on the customer's shoulders. If the customer caused the problem and knows it, he or she often feels exonerated if given a part in solving the problem.

CORDs: The Solution Space Context

As was obvious with the auto repair example, good problem solutions are often very context or situational bound. Customer-oriented response dimensions (CORDs) reflect the situational nature of Solution Spaces by imbedding them in a grid or matrix that reflects that situation.

There are at least *two* dimensions to most recovery situations:

- The origin of the problem (who caused it)
- The status or impact of the customer involved (who is complaining)

Goal	• Fix the problem. • Regain customer trust. • Save the account.
Tactic	• Show concern for customer. • Support the relationship. • Evidence prompt and effective action.

Example

We fail to credit deposit properly. Several checks are returned ISF to credit card and mortgage companies.

- Apologize to the customer.
- Credit account immediately.
- Check for other returned items.
- Get list of organizations involved.
- Phone and write, cc: customer.
- Follow-up phone calls(s); inform of status.

Figure 9-1. A "we did it" Solution Space with imbedded guidance.

Goal	• Help fix the problem. • Exhibit value-added assistance. • Minimize customer distress.
Tactic	• Show concern for customer. • Assist customer in fixing problem. • Evidence concern for customer discomfort/embarrassment.

Example

Customer failed to endorse check deposited via ATM over the weekend. Several checks written for large amounts.

- Call customer.
- Verify deposit.
- Arrange for endorsement.
- Issue hold request for checks that have been written.
- Explain procedures to customer.

Figure 9-2. A "customer error" Solution Space with imbedded example.

Who Did It?

There are just four dimensions of culpability or causation:

1. **We did it.** The organization made a mistake that upset, injured, or inconvenienced the customer.

2. **Customer did it.** The customer made a mistake, broke the product, failed to do, or did something that caused the problem, upset, or inconvenience.

3. **Third party did it.** A third party—shipper, subcontractor, customer's dog—did something to bring about the upset, injury, or inconvenience.

4. **Act of nature.** The upset, injury, or inconvenience was caused by a storm, earthquake, famine, or flood—something beyond anyone's control.

NOTE: Some would suggest that causes 3 and 4 are essentially the same. We disagree. A storm or earthquake cannot be enlisted to help solve the problem, but an errant independent shipper or third party can be.

Type of Customer

Although all customers demand—and deserve—to be treated with respect and dignity and are owed redress for their problems and inconvenience, it also is true that not all customers

have the same long-term value to the organization. Most organizations have customers who are so important that a loss of their business would be a hardship, if not a catastrophe. And most have "loss-leader" customers whose value is marginal at best. And most organizations triage their recovery treatment on that basis to some extent. Creating a Solution Space matrix based on that principle may be uncomfortable, but it simply makes obvious and codifies what is already being done. For instance, airlines expect cabin crew to treat million-miler frequent business travelers differently than occasional vacation fliers. It is important to make those expectations clear.

The CORDs matrix in Figure 9-3 has the four culpability or cause conditions across the horizontal and a hypothetical customer typology along the vertical. In this instance, there are four customer classifications from "high net worth" at the top of the scale to "transient" (meaning non-account holding, occasional customer) at the bottom. It has been our experience that some organizations, on realizing that they have a significant number of de facto customers of type one classification, decide to collapse their matrix to a more manageable number. Some, because of concerns for the way such a classification could be interpreted from outside the organization, collapse the type of customer classifications to just two or three: customer/noncustomer, or high net customer/average customer/noncustomer. However you decide to deal with this dimension, it is important for your associates to know if there is to be differential recovery treatment by customer type, and, if there is, what the appropriate distinctions are.

Creating Effective Solution Spaces within the CORDs Matrix

The best Solution Spaces do not come from thin air or a fertile imagination. They are researched and refined by in-house experts—you and your CSR team. Here is one approach.

1. Have a representative group of your CSRs log their customer problem calls and encounters for 1 to 2 months. They should record the problem, the solution, and the customer's reaction to, and/or apparent satisfaction with, the solution.

	Customer Error	Our Error	Third Party	Act of Nature
High-Net Worth Customer	• Show concern for customer. • Assist customer in fixing problem. • Evidence concern for customer discomfort/ embarrassment. • Call customer. • Verify deposit. • Arrange for endorsement. • Issue hold request for checks that have been written. • Explain procedures to customer.			
Active Customer with Multiple Accounts		• Show concern for customer. • Support the relationship. • Evidence prompt and effective action. • Apologize to customer. • Credit account ASAP. • Check for other returned items. • Get list of organizations involved. • Phone, write, cc. customer. • Follow-up.		
Active Customer with Single Account				
Transient Customer				

Type of Customer (vertical axis label)

Figure 9-3. Customer-oriented response dimensions or Solution Space matrix.

2. When you have amassed a quantity of problem examples (we suggest shooting for 100 so you are sure to have captured the entire field of most frequent examples), transfer the information from log form to 3- by 5-inch cards, with one problem/solution/outcome per card.

3. Sort the problem into piles corresponding to the categories on your CORDs matrix. If, for example, you have decided to use the four culpability categories and three customer type categories, you would have twelve piles of problem cards.

4. Work with each of the twelve piles. Sort the cards into groups of like problems.

5. Edit the piles of like problems for consistency and appropriateness of solution.

6. Now comes the creative part. Look through the solutions and problems.

- What are the common characteristics of the effective solutions?
- What guidelines accurately reflect the way the CSRs approached the problem—and the customer—to come to an effective solution?

7. Create a Solution Space similar to those in figures 9-1 and 9-2. Pick one of the problems to use as the Solution Space exemplar.

8. Retain the entire problem card pile that went into creating the Solution Space for use in training.

9. Repeat the process for the remaining piles. Call it your CORDs matrix.

NOTE: Some organizations add a third dimension to the mix: the emotional state of the customer. Irate, frightened, or outraged customers are indeed "different" and require "different " handling than customers who are simply unconvinced or mildly annoyed. Whether these differences are a significant enough overlay to warrant adding the complexity of a third dimension to your CORDs matrix is of unclear, if not dubious, apparent value for helping associates create effective service recovery.

10

Apology to Atonement:

The Anatomy of Great Grovel

A few words of regret is a way of saying you care, a show of sensitivity to the ragged edges of another's emotion.

—Robert Conklin
Author, How to Get People to Do Things

The "cycle of contrition" that flows from apology to atonement is an ancient and honored tradition. In the Anglo-Saxon culture, this language of remorse ranges from an indifferent shrug of the shoulders and a half-mumbled "sorry" to extravagant gestures of extreme and showy repentance.

Organizations mired in service mediocrity give little thought to either the proper form or potential power of "grovel"—apology and atonement—done well. Most relegate it to an ill-funded, poorly positioned staff unit made up of ex-debutantes whose core competence is planning parties and writing thank-you notes. Other organizations are slow to recognize how today's customer can quickly spot counterfeit concern and imitation humility. It also pays to remember that, for most customers, a grumpy refund still beats a smiling rebuff.

Grovel management requires far more than drafting apology letters or randomly administering some form of monetary recompense to particularly persistent or pesky customers. It is, or can be, a key strategic element of an effective recovery process. Winning organizations seem to effortlessly turn mayhem into magic, leaving customers awed by the process and healed by the gesture, with their loyalty restored, if not amplified. Our work with and observations of these winning organizations suggest that two factors stand at the core of healing a broken relationship: (1) the proper grovel prescription and (2) the proper grovel dosage.

The Proper Grovel Prescription

The following three questions provide guidance in making the best strategic decisions when it comes to choosing grovel approaches and building atonement prescriptions for your customer-oriented response dimensions (CORDs) matrix.

1. **What does our customer research indicate will be the best grovel mechanism for the** *"average"* **customer?**

Consider the experience of Domino's Pizza. When Domino's first launched the pizza delivery business, it wanted "on-time" delivery to be its touchstone and signature feature.

Because the average pizza delivery time was around 30 minutes, management chose that standard as part of its marketplace promise, "Delivery in 30 minutes or your pizza is free."

Although the pledge achieved Domino's advertising and marketing goals, the number of customers who took them up on the guarantee was far less than the number of "more than 30 minute" deliveries.

Focus groups yielded the explanation. Most customers thought "free pizza" was excessive atonement for a pizza arriving 5 or 10 minutes late. When Domino's shifted its guarantee to $3 off the pizza price if delivered beyond 30 minutes, a far greater number of customers took them up on the guarantee. The price discount proved much closer to customers' expectations of fair recompense.

Follow Dominos' lead: Conduct some customer research to get a sense of what your customers believe should happen as a result of service breakdowns. That will help you better match your atonement to customer expectations.

2. What does *this* particular customer (or type of customer) expect?

As mentioned before, service recovery should be personalized. Although understanding the "average" customer will help you establish general recovery standards and guidance for front-line people, the "unique" or quirky customer may have different notions about what constitutes appropriate recovery. Atonement, after all, is in the eye of the beholder, and the requirement for grovel will vary depending on the mood, makeup, and unique tapestry of problems experienced by the customer.

This makes picking the right approach to atonement as much art as science, and often it necessitates customer input, as in "What can I do to make it up to you?" It also suggests your front-line service providers should be trained, coached, and rewarded to be dramatic listeners and lavish understanders. Finally, it means your unit or organization should provide clear guidance on what is reasonable restitution in a wide assortment of recovery scenarios. If the diagnostic question is popped and the customer retorts sarcastically, "If you really want me to be happy, I'd like free dry-cleaning for me—and for everyone who attended my twentieth high-school reunion—for a full year," the last thing you need is a compliant employee scrambling to fulfill the most outlandish of the requests.

3. **What recovery approaches best communicate your unit or organization's vision, values, and style?**

Recovery needs to fit. Although you want customers to be surprised and delighted by your response, it is important they think, "That's in line with what I'd expect this organization to do." If the customer is left puzzled, your choice of atonement probably has not hit the mark. Recovery should be in sync with the kind of organization you are striving to be (your vision) as well as the kind of organization you are when you are at your best (your values). Although vision and value lend depth to your response, your organization's style gives recovery a unique definition. Ritz-Carlton would choose a recovery response that is classy and elegant; the Residence Inn might chose atonement that is more folksy and family oriented. The "style" befits the overall tone and tenor of the organization.

The Proper Grovel Dosage

There is apology and then there is APOLOGY. Having chosen the atonement prescription, the next task is to determine how high to turn the rheostat, how formal or how low key to be in your apology. For example, if you decide on atonement in the form of monetary recompense (cash), the the next decision is, "how much?" A bank we know set the following atonement policy, "If there is an error in your statement, we will refund you double the service charge," and it got little more than a ho-hum reaction from most customers. But when that bank upped the ante to "no service charge for a year" for such errors, it not only captured customer attention, but also the attention of the local media.

Three questions provide guidance in choosing the right "grovel dosage."

1. Do you want *this* action to make a statement to *this* particular customer?

Sometimes it is important to amplify atonement to make it more special for certain (read: highly valued) customers. An automobile dealership might use this decision tree, for instance, to provide loaner cars to customers dropping off their regular vehicles for repair:

- For "periodic" customers bringing in cars for routine maintenance, a dependable used loaner
- For customers who have experienced problems that were not fixed right the first time or otherwise should not have occurred, a standard line of new vehicle
- For the particularly loyal or valued customer, a top-of-the-line new car as a loaner whenever they come in for service work

Similarly, a credit card customer might call a bank complaining about the escalating annual fee. On investigation, a customer service specialist finds the customer has held the card for 10 years, keeps a healthy card balance, pays the minimum due each month, and has checking, savings, and line-of-credit accounts with the bank. With the big picture in mind, she decides to either waive or dramatically reduce the fee rather than risk losing the sum of the customer's business. For a customer of less long-term value, the customer service representative would more likely stand firm on the fee increase.

2. Do you want this action to make a particular statement to your *employees*?

There are times when the actions taken after service breakdowns are chosen less for customers and more as a statement to your employees. For example, an oil drilling supply and service company learned that one of its key customers had experienced a problem with one of its oil drills. The $20 part gave out far before its expected life span and was not kept in stock by the customer. Under ordinary conditions—for a less valuable customer, perhaps—the company would send the needed part overnight for next-day delivery. However, the owner wanted to send a message to his workforce that this customer was special. He asked an employee to fly with the part that evening for an in-person delivery to the customer, spend the night, and return the next day. Total cost of the atonement? More than $500. In the owner's eyes, it was a small price to pay for this valued customer's continued loyalty. The gesture was an important genuflection to the importance of the relationship.

3. Do you need this action for particular strategic positioning (defensively or offensively)?

A customer of Starbucks Coffee purchased an expensive espresso machine for himself and one as a wedding gift for a friend. Before long, the customer claimed his machine had stopped working, and the friend who received the gift found his was rusted and some parts were missing. The customer complained, returned the coffee makers, and requested replacements of higher value as recompense. Starbucks' representatives denied the one machine was rusted, explaining that each coffee maker is field tested before being sold and that water residue occasionally causes a small film of rust that can be easily removed. But the company did counter with an offer of loaner machines until the two were repaired (not the luxury models the customer wanted), an apology, and some small gifts. Not satisfied, the frustrated customer took out a full-page ad in the *Wall Street Journal*, seeking others who had experienced problems with Starbucks. When he received several thousand responses to an 800 number included with the ad, he became an instant media darling. Starbucks refused to budge from its stance, causing the customer to take out another full-page ad.

There came a point as this very public back-and-forth dragged on when a dramatic recovery, regardless of who was right or wrong, quite possibly could have nipped the situation in the bud and short circuited the media coverage. Had Starbucks performed a high visibility act of recovery after the customer's first ad ran to turn the situation in its favor, the customer would have lost his audience and the situation might have become far less public and damaging to Starbucks' reputation. (For more details on the specifics of the Starbucks case, see Chapter 12 on Crisis Intervention.)

There are times like these when recovery needs to serve a strategic purpose, either offensively (to shorten the life span of a potentially difficult situation or lingering negative PR) or defensively (to quell an already escalating situation). Beyond pride or ego, companies need to realize that, in some cases, recovery is more about strategic positioning, positive public relations, and the goodwill that result from large acts of atonement than it is about who is right or wrong or about whose motives are pure and whose are tainted.

11

Recovering from Recovery:

Turning Spendthrifts into "Passionate Pragmatists"

Nothing is ever gained by winning an argument and losing a customer.

—Anonymous

Sue was new to her role as hotel concierge and eager to live up to the lofty service expectations of the job. The customer had called the reservation clerk at the New York hotel a week before and confirmed that his reserved rooms would be ready by 3 P.M., which was crucial because it was the only time an important client could come by to review a research report the guest had prepared.

On learning that the rooms would not be ready until 4 P.M., the panicked customer turned to the concierge desk and Sue.

"We need your help. The reservationist promised us rooms by 3 P.M., our client is already en route, and we can't very well meet in the lobby. We need a quiet and private place to discuss a very sensitive report."

The concierge, biting at the bit to demonstrate her new prowess, swung into action. "I can give you our best suite. I'll have a bottle of wine delivered to your room along with three glasses. Oh, and one more thing . . . dinner for you and your client will be on the house tonight in our restaurant."

The concierge obviously meant well but had overreacted. Instead of being pleased, the customer was stunned. He asked Sue just to provide one regular room and one suite, cancel the wine before it arrived, and then opted to have dinner at a restaurant—one of his customer's choosing—outside the hotel. Sue's overzealous response made the customer's minor problem seem even smaller. It was not small in actuality; it was just small when put beside the extravagant action she set in motion. The customer could discern no business reason for her way-way-way beyond-the-call-of-duty action. And he honestly felt bad for the organization, which, had he been in a greedy mood, would have been forced to pick up the tab for Sue's overly lavish gesture.

What can a supervisor or manager do to reign in such overzealous recovery without being seen as an overseer who

must approve every transaction? What steps help prevent atonement so out of proportion to the service breakdown experienced that the customer is embarrassed or uncomfortable? How do you constrain extravagance without squelching a sincere zeal to serve?

Here are five ideas:

1. **Teach 'em the business.** People make smart recovery decisions if they know what "smartness" means. Help front-line service people think like owners by making them "business literate." Front liners need to know the cost of doing business, understand the balance sheet, be able to read a profit and loss statement, and have up-to-date information on how the business is performing. More important, they need daily data that clearly relate their specific actions and decisions to the unit bottom line.

Ritz-Carlton Hotels gives housekeepers the authority to spend up to $2,000 to ensure guests leave with a positive feeling about the hotel. That may seem like a wide berth, but the housekeepers do not give away the store. Before granted that freedom to spend, they are educated about the financial impact of their decisions and in what problem scenarios—and with what types of customers—it makes sense to spend the upper end of that limit. Ritz-Carlton also has built a culture where employees feel as protective of the company as they do of the customer. Remember, empowerment does not mean unlimited license. It means responsible freedom: finding the right balance of "go the extra mile" service and "take care of the organization" stewardship.

2. **Provide guidance, not just "go get 'em!"** The charge to "do whatever it takes" can backfire unless directives are coupled with direction. When managers tell employees "you're empowered" but provide little or no guidance, employees either assume a risk-averse position out of a fear of making a major blunder, or they respond like the hotel concierge in our earlier example and turn what should have been reasonable atonement into unreasonable wastefulness. Empowered ignorance is the breeding ground for anarchy. Empowerment without enablement—telling your people to "do whatever it takes" but then pulling the

ball away from them, Lucy-to-Charlie-Brown style, as soon as they make an empowered decision you do not like, or failing to give them the proper training in making good decisions—can create frustration on the front lines.

Devote time in staff meetings to identifying the most common customer disappointments in your unit and brainstorm some ways to atone appropriately. After ideas and recovery "decision trees" are generated, critique the options and build the most effective into your training manuals or job aids. Be clear on examples that fall outside the range of what you consider appropriate. And make sure to praise creative solutions that also are frugal. Let employees know that, although they need to serve the customer's interests, they also need to keep one eye on your organization's bottom line.

3. **Make heroes of service people who mix passion with pragmatism.** Make heroes of people who perform recovery in ways that reflect responsible pragmatism, who provide "just enough" atonement to put the organization back in the customer's good graces, and who do it in ways that leave no doubt they care about the customer's experience. Be sure to tell the recovery story when recognizing or affirming these heroes. Your people need to know the "why" as well as the "whom" behind such lauded actions. Role models who emulate good service as well as good stewardship give your front liners a clear standard to shoot for.

It is important that creativity be part of the criteria for affirmation. The last thing you want is to endlessly reward the same recovery approach to the same situation. Although recovery can be effectively planned, it can never be effectively canned. Customers want to feel their situation is unique and that your response to their problem reflects that uniqueness.

4. **Involve your people in service breakdown analysis.** Good recovery involves effective problem solving and the ultimate elimination or radical reduction of root causes that lead to customer disappointment. Customers, impressed with spectacular recovery, are less enthralled when they repeatedly encounter

the same service breakdown. It is important employees see their role as problem solvers, not just damage controllers.

Consider devoting a part of every staff meeting to having employees identify one problem area that results in all-too-frequent customer disappointment. Have them outline what happens, how customers react, and what actions typically are taken (or not taken) to mollify the customer. Use tools common to continuous improvement or total quality initiatives—brainstorming, cross-functional process analysis, pareto (80-20) method, frequency charting, or fishbone diagrams—to try and unravel the true drivers of service breakdown.

Brainstorm ways to eliminate the causes, assign responsibility for corrective action or follow-up with other departments that might be contributing to recurring problems, and plan for a follow-up review at the next staff meeting.

5. **Transfer the spendthrifts to a noncontact role.** The final step, one you hopefully will not have to take after exploring the previous suggestions, is to place front liners who repeatedly go overboard in recovery responses into non-customer-contact roles. Chances are their misguided eagerness will be more effectively channeled in positions with fewer negative consequences to the organization.

In many cases, you will find these people are severe "conflict avoiders" with great fears of rejection. They will do anything to prevent having to disappoint a customer and are more likely than others to acquiesce to unreasonable demands. Other such spendthrifts see their mission in life as "do-gooders" at the organization's expense. The attitude is manifest in statements such as, "Here, take two. This deep-pocketed company will never miss it. Besides, you seem like a nice person." Even if customers view the gesture as a positive, they often come away with an uneasy worry about how such wanton generosity, played out many times over, will affect the long-term viability of the organization. Not to mention what keeping such employees in high-visibility, high-impact customer-contact roles says about the business acumen or attentiveness of your company's top management team.

12

Crisis Intervention

I believe that if you are honest and straightforward with customers, they will treat you like a neighbor when circumstances beyond your control put you in a `one-down` position.

—Milton Moore
General Manager, Vision Cable

Beyond the workaday recovery challenges of disappearing luggage, overcooked filet mignon, and phones that go dead mid-call, there exists another galaxy of problems where the stakes are considerably higher. A realm where adept recovery can mean the difference between industrial-strength market share and a free-falling stock price. An arena where lack of forethought and pre-planning lead to becoming a regular punch line on "The Tonight Show" and to a crippling loss of public trust in your organization. The dreaded world of a major service or product crisis.

Crisis situations demand an escalated level of recovery response. When a product is tampered with, contaminated food sickens customers, a computer system crashes, a tanker spills, or a U.S. president is caught in an indelicate position, recovery skills are put to the ultimate test. These situations differ from run-of-the-mill recovery fire fighting by "hyperextending" the capabilities of your organization. They demand extensive resource availability, clear and firm executive decision making, and rapid response. And they often bring that dreaded force—the media—into play.

Yet, just like everyday service recovery, an effectively managed crisis can leave your organization looking stronger after the disaster than before. A crisis, handled well, puts on display for customers, employees, investors, and sometimes the world at large the integrity, shrewd decision making, and preparedness of your top management team. And that increased visibility and name recognition can, in the long term, help boost customer confidence and esteem.

Like service recovery, crisis management requires a coordinated, well-thought-out, multifunctional effort that is in place far before disaster strikes and continues after the damage has been contained. Organizations that believe they can "wing it" through crisis situations by relying on the quick thinking and wherewithal of top management or view accidents simply as a "cost of doing business" usually end up with severely wounded franchises and as the eviscerated subjects of "how to mismanage crisis" case studies and press "special investigations."

Not all crises come in the form of threat to life and limb, of course, nor are they always as headline-grabbing as the Exxon Valdez spill or Challenger space shuttle disaster. Sometimes crisis arrives as threats to the company's reputation, integrity, or ability to continue to serve customers: computer system crashes, major product delays, poor financial performance or mismanagement, labor disputes, extended power outages, or rumors about your company erupting on the Internet. These are events that may not show up in the newspapers but are clearly visible on customers' or shareholders' radar screens.

Crisis often falls into three categories:

1. Crisis of nuisance
2. Crisis of integrity
3. Crisis of catastrophe

Crisis of Nuisance

When problems that, under typical conditions or organizational response, might simply be irritating to customers escalate to the unbelievably annoying or inconvenient, or when a seemingly small service breakdown mushrooms into a full-blown public relations disaster fueled by customers with an acute sense of being wronged, a serious case of persistence, media savvy, or deep pockets, you have a crisis of nuisance. Executives at Starbucks Coffee know the territory all too well.

In 1995, a Starbucks customer named Jeremy Dorosin walked into a Starbucks coffee shop in Berkeley, California, and purchased a $299 Italian espresso maker for himself and a $169 machine as a wedding gift for a friend. When Dorosin's coffee maker broke down and he learned that his friend's gift machine had arrived rusted and with some parts missing, he was not whistling Dixie. What's more, according to a report in the *Wall Street Journal*, when he asked for the free half-pound of coffee the store usually includes with coffee maker purchases, a cashier refused. When Dorosin suggested a free cup of cappuccino instead, he claims that also was shot down, in very rude fashion.

Dorosin says when he initially complained, Starbucks downplayed his grievances. On the other hand, Starbucks, which prides itself on customer relations, says it offered loaner machines until his machines were repaired, some small gifts, and an apology. Company representatives denied the machine was incomplete or rusted; they said it appeared to be used, because Starbucks tests the machines before selling them to ensure they are working.

The recovery effort did not satisfy Dorosin. He asked that his inconvenienced friend be sent a deluxe, top-of-the line Starbucks espresso machine as recompense instead—this had been a wedding gift, after all. Starbucks refused, calling the request unreasonable. The company also refused to send the next nicest machine, a $450 model, but it offered to refund Dorosin's money or to substitute two other espresso makers.

Dorosin again balked, and his next move was an eye-opener: He took out an ad in the northern California edition of the *Wall Street Journal* that screamed, "Had any problems at Starbucks Coffee? You're not alone. Interested? Let's talk." Included was an 800 number to call. The next week, Dorosin, who claimed he had never before made a consumer complaint, bought an even larger version of the ad in the *Wall Street Journal*. He claimed to have received more than 3,000 calls and letters and to have spent $10,000 on the whole effort.

Starbucks responded to the ads by sending two $269 espresso machines, two pounds of coffee, a steaming pitcher, condiment shakers, cups and saucers, a $30 refund, and letters of apology. But Dorosin refused the delivery—too little, too late, he said. His last demand: a two-page apology from Starbucks printed in the *Wall Street Journal*, estimated cost of $247,182, that would admit having sold Dorosin a used machine. So that "some good could come" of the situation, he also suggested Starbucks establish a center for runaway children in San Francisco.

Starbucks' CEO told the *Seattle Post-Intelligencer* that meeting Dorosin's latest demands would not be "responsible" and said Dorosin is "mad at the world and wants to take it out on us." Through the course of the brouhaha, company spokespeople repeatedly told the press that "we did all we could to resolve this, but his demands are unreasonable."

Some damage, however, had already been done to Starbucks' reputation and integrity. As the situation wore on, it played out in countless newspapers and media outlets across the country.

Might the coffee giant have handled the crisis better, or was it justified in its response to an opportunistic—and insatiable—customer? As the situation escalated, right or wrong became moot; public perception was now Starbucks' greatest foe. Conclusions from a study of the case by professors at Thomas More College and Miami University, published in the *Case Research Journal*, suggest Starbucks should have realized earlier in the conflict that Dorosin bordered on zealot and that he was willing to spend time, effort, and money far beyond the average upset customer in pursuing the problem. Case authors believe his placing ads in the *Wall Street Journal* and his other "increasingly strident requirements" could have been anticipated and avoided.

"The company appeared to underestimate his resolve, misunderstand his intentions, and made atonement offers which were parsimonious and short-sighted," they write. "Even if Dorosin's original complaint was false, and even if he did demand a $2,495 machine, the damage to the company in terms of adverse publicity, executive time, and expense far outweighed the cost of giving in."

Often the only way a company can dig out of a public relations hole like this is through dramatic gesture. As a company with significant resources, Starbucks could have created an apology and atonement so large and unexpected that it would have blown both Dorosin and the snickering press away, and it would have made a lasting impression on its customer base. With its deep pockets, it could have, for instance, bought out the seating for a San Francisco Giants baseball game, declared the evening Jeremy Dorosin night, and made admission a food gift appropriate for stocking at an area homeless center or food shelf pantry.

Crisis of Integrity

Sometimes an organization's integrity is called into question; and customer, employee, and shareholder confidence sways in the balance. Whether it is customers claiming you have not lived up to promises or stood behind policy or charges that your organization has stepped beyond moral or ethical boundaries, there is serious repair to be done to make the company "whole" again and restore public trust.

The supermarket chain Food Lion found its integrity questioned a few years ago when it was accused by ABC-TV's *Prime Time Live* of knowingly selling spoiled meat. The company's

stock went into free fall, landing at about half its preinvestigative report value. But Food Lion executives did not give up or wallow in defensiveness. Experts credit them with a strong and swift reaction. Food Lion began offering public tours of its stores, putting large windows in meat preparation areas, improving lighting, expanding employee training, and offering discounts to lure wary customers back into stores. Before long, the Food and Drug Administration had given Food Lion its coveted "excellent" rating, and sales began climbing back.

Northwest Airlines also tread portions of this ground during a record snowstorm at its Detroit hub in January 1999, and it showed a few fissures in its crisis management planning along the way. In the middle of a storm that convinced other air carriers to cut back or discontinue service to airports throughout the midwest, Minneapolis-based Northwest made an ill-fated decision to let thirty planes land at the Detroit airport. The result, as reported in the *Wall Street Journal* and other media outlets around the globe, was an out-and-out mess.

The thirty planes and thousands of passengers inside had to sit on the airport tarmac for as long as 8 hours because other Northwest jets were tying up the gates. The situation was so bad that one group of passengers filed a lawsuit in Wayne County, Michigan, against Northwest and the Detroit airport. They alleged that thousands of passengers were "imprisoned" on Northwest's planes during the storm and not allowed to disembark for hours. The plaintiffs reported there was no food or water available, toilets were backed up and overflowing, and people were forced to urinate into cups. Indeed, the *Wall Street Journal* story said that one Northwest captain used his cockpit phone to call John Dasburg, Northwest's CEO, at home and declare the situation desperate. What was Northwest's principal recovery response? Some pilots tried to calm passengers who had been trapped in the glorified metal boxes for hours by showing movies.

In the aftermath of the snowstorm, Northwest said it could not get the planes out of the gates because the airport was not being plowed fast enough. Airline officials also charged that the airport plowing crews did not work fast enough or in the right sequence and that the crews inadvertently created giant snow walls that trapped planes at the gate. But Northwest officials later conceded that they had made a mistake in bringing the thirty flights into Detroit, instead of holding them at their origins or diverting them to airports outside the snow belt.

Although it might be tempting to write the problem off to an "uncontrollable"—Mother Nature unloading both barrels over a holiday—the reality is United and American Airlines, operating out of Chicago's O'Hare airport, did not experience the customer outrage Northwest did in Detroit, even though Chicago's airport received many more inches of snow and handled far more air traffic in the same stretch. Both American and United—showing evidence of good disaster preparedness and decision making— had canceled most of their flights on Saturday and Sunday.

Some good did emerge from the fiasco, however. In the aftermath, Northwest announced a new policy to remove passengers from inbound flights if the delayed airplane does not reach a gate within 1 hour. Now if passengers become stranded on inbound planes, reports the *Minneapolis Star Tribune*, the captain of a Northwest flight has the authority to activate an "event recovery plan" that includes procedures to remove the passengers from the delayed aircraft in a timely manner. One new tool that will be used is "air stairs" that can be wheeled up to a delayed plane for passenger departure; Northwest is acquiring the stairs for twelve airports. The customer service plan also includes upgraded training for all of the carrier's front-line managers and employees.

Ripples from Northwest's stranded-passenger disaster were felt across the entire airline industry. Many credit the situation with persuading all major U.S. carriers to come together behind a new industry customer service plan, "Customers First," designed to stop a movement in Congress toward a new "passenger bill of rights." Included among the many "voluntary" pledges is one to make every reasonable effort to provide food, water, and rest room facilities for on-board passengers who are on the ground for extended periods.

Crisis of Catastrophe

Catastrophe can emerge from nowhere at any time. One need not look deep into the history books for evidence. Two sky-walks collapsing in the Kansas City Hyatt Regency Hotel, a lethal gas leak at Union Carbide's Bhopal plant in India, the Exxon Valdez oil spill, and the more recent Alaska Air flight disaster are but a few examples.

In other cases, catastrophe is not yet manifest but looms as real threat: accusations that cellular phones cause brain tumors, tampons might cause toxic-shock syndrome, or prolonged exposure to asbestos is tied to lung diseases.

More common than those headline-grabbing catastrophes are missteps that do not endanger life or limb but rather organizational or customer well-being. Financial losses from corrupted or sabotaged databases, voice mail systems that crash and send current messages floating away into the ethers, and utility power outages can damage customer trust and erode business.

How do you prepare for the unthinkable? For the potentially devastating crises caused by anything from sabotage, to errant employees, to Mother Nature?

Johnson & Johnson's handling of its Tylenol crisis remains the enduring benchmark for managing catastrophe and emerging stronger as a result.

In 1982, seven people in Illinois died after ingesting cyanide-laced Tylenol. A few years later, another person in New York was poisoned and died. Responding swiftly, Johnson & Johnson quickly canceled all Tylenol television advertising, activated a toll-free telephone hotline to answer consumer questions, and offered refunds or exchanges to customers who had purchased Tylenol capsules. The company then announced it would no longer sell any of its over-the-counter drugs in capsule form, a decision that cost it millions of dollars but that sent a clear message to consumers.

The Chicago poisonings caused Tylenol's share of the painkiller market to free fall from 35 to 7 percent overnight. But Johnson & Johnson staged what industry experts called a "miracle" comeback when executives took rapid and forceful measures to ensure public safety and restore trust in the company's top-selling product. With full-page ads and television spots announcing its intentions, the company spent an estimated $300 million to recall thirty-one million old packages of Tylenol capsules and promote new ones that were tri-sealed to resist tampering. They also courageously stuck by their brand name rather than retiring it, as many PR experts suggested they do.

The company's stock price began moving upward not long after, and within 3 months it had regained 95 percent of its pre-crisis market share.

How did Johnson & Johnson come out of this torture chamber more highly regarded after the catastrophe than before? Management experts credit much of it to executives' close alignment of corporate values and behavior. Looking down the barrel of lethal product tampering, Johnson & Johnson's senior leaders quickly turned to their crisis management manifesto, "safety over profit." That document, which instructed executive decisions in far less stressful times, was the company's guiding star for the Tylenol disaster. Company executives also did not spend time pointing fingers or reacting defensively. Nor did they hesitate to make the financially costly decision to recall the product or to go immediately into production with a discernibly different and obviously more tamperproof product.

Tips for Good Crisis Management

Many organizations believe they are practicing good crisis management when in reality they are only "cleaning up a mess" once a crisis has occurred. Whether you are hit with a crisis of integrity, nuisance, or catastrophe, your odds of emerging stronger in the aftermath will increase if you use some core crisis planning and management principles, according to *Organizational Dynamics*, a publication of the American Management Association:

- **A crisis plan should be guided by values ingrained in the culture.** The values should address the organization's priorities (Johnson & Johnson's or Proctor & Gamble's "safety over profit" with the Tylenol and Rely tampon scares), the needs of its most important stakeholders (stockholders, employees, customers), and the responsibility of individual employees (to know and act on the values that, for instance, the interests of customers come first). Organization-wide clarity about values goes far in guiding decision making during crisis periods.

When Odwalla, a California-based fresh juice company, was identified as a possible source of *Escherichia coli* bacteria, the company's value system drove its crisis response. Integral to that response was constant communication with customers about developments and decisions made throughout the scare.

- **Preplanned responses to an assortment of crisis scenarios.** The most dangerous crisis is one that "blind sides" a company and forces deer-in-the-headlights reactions from executives or company spokespeople. Even your top troubleshooters or public relations spin doctors can lose their ability to think objectively when hit out of the blue. And most executives, tunnel-visioned into making the numbers for the upcoming quarter, do not spend much time looking down the road or scanning the environment for potential crisis.

  Although some disasters simply cannot be planned for, experts recommend you leave no stone unturned. Alaska Airlines believed it had an airtight emergency plan when one of its jets hit a mountain in Alaska. The crisis plan was highly detailed, assigning specific roles to airline personnel on its crisis teams. But the airline did not—some say could not—anticipate that relatives would want to charter their own helicopters and fly to the crash site. Airline officials had to politely and sensitively inform the relatives that the National Transportation Safety Board would not allow that.

- **Planning that addresses each stage of a crisis life cycle.** Most crises develop, escalate, and subside in a five-phase sequence: (1) signal or "warning sign" detection, (2) preparation, (3) damage control, (4) recovery, and (5) applying lessons learned. Your crisis planning should address each stage.

In *signal detection*, you proactively scan for warning signals of potential crisis. Many catastrophes or near-tragedies are compound failures that built up over time from seemingly isolated, benign problems. TransAmerica Life, for instance, makes a point of scrutinizing and probing its operations and environment for potential crisis, and sophisticated screening devices help detect potential fraud. Other companies regularly examine data from help desks or customer service areas for early hints of a gathering storm, such as steadily increasing tech support calls.

Preparation requires that top leaders adopt a crisis management mind-set, create a crisis management team, and do run-throughs of hypothetical incidents. In *damage control*, where the bulk of most crisis management efforts go, companies attempt to keep the crisis from spreading and to stop the hemorrhaging.

Recovery is when short- and long-term plans are put in place to resume normal business operations. For instance, when a fire gutted its Los Angeles headquarters, First Interstate Bank was able, because of advance planning, to quickly relocate to a competitor's facility. Rather than losing days or weeks of service, customers faced delays of just a few hours. The last phase, *applying lessons learned*, includes unearthing, assessing, and reflecting on lessons from the crisis experience to apply to future problems. Many executives miss the opportunity to learn, because their primary goal is to point fingers or simply distance themselves from the crisis.

- **Honesty over evasiveness.** What happens if your crisis hits the headlines? Nothing stops the media's feeding frenzy faster than signs that a crisis situation is under control, and that is often a result of a solid disaster communications plan. Some companies set up corporate SWAT teams to communicate with the media, customers, shareholders, and others during crisis. Dow Chemical, for instance, created a twenty-page manifesto for communicating with the public during a disaster, all the way down to who was going to run the copy machines, reports *Time* magazine. Others prepare by using the expert advice of public relations firms.

How forthright should you be with the media and your core constituencies? Many executives who have been through the fire suggest erring on the side of overdisclosure, arguing that credibility in many of these situations is more important than protecting your legal back side. Warren Buffet, who had some experience with crisis situations himself, gave this advice to the *Harvard Business Review*, "First state clearly that you don't know all the facts. Then promptly state the facts you do know. One's objective should be to get it right, get it quick, get it out and get it over. You see, your problem won't improve with age."

Denial, or failing to acknowledge the gravity of the situation upon you, is one of the biggest threats to good crisis management and usually triggers a vicious domino effect. Other times, ignorance or poor internal communication is the problem. H.J. Heinz found that out in the 1980s, when its Star-Kist subsidiary was accused of shipping one million cans of rancid tuna in Canada. Even after the Canadian prime minister impounded the fish, Heinz executives chose to bury their heads in the sand and refused to speak to the press or the public. A company spokesman claimed ignorance; he said top management truly did not know how the problem had happened. Soon after, Heinz developed its own emergency crisis management team.

Three numbers serve as important milestones when communicating during a crisis, suggests *Communication World* magazine: 60, 3, and 1. Within 60 minutes of being notified of a crisis, especially a natural or environmental disaster, initial communication should be distributed, indicating what is known about the situation and what response steps are under way. Within 3 hours, a crisis communication team should be in place, even if it is bare bones and awaiting arrival of reinforcements. And, by the end of day 1 of the crisis, a short-term communication plan should be in place that specifies key messages and facts, identifies spokespeople, and indicates the next day's needs.

- **A plan isn't enough—you've gotta practice, too.** A highly detailed plan—on paper—is only step one in helping your organization out of crisis. True preparedness means putting your organization through role-playing exercises, simulations, structured walkthroughs, and drills. No one knows that better than Exxon and the oil industry in the wake of the Valdez disaster. Responding to circumstances surrounding the spill, Congress passed legislation that mandates oil shippers must conduct emergency response exercises at least twice a year.

When it comes to crisis, experts say there are only two pertinent categories: those who have had them and those who will. But take heart; if the companies we have been discussing here can look into the jaws of disaster and survive, even thrive, so can you and your organization.

Part Four
Leading Service Recovery

We have a belief that our guests will only receive the kind of treatment we want them to receive if the cast members receive that same kind of treatment from their managers.

—Walt Disney World Handbook

Effective service recovery happens at the intersection of high tech and high touch, that place where two key elements come together to return smiles and confidence to your customers' face and pace:

- A *"recovery friendly" system*—the hardware, software, and communications technology—and the policies, procedures and permissions—that make it easy for customers to report problems and for employees to efficiently solve them.

117

- *Recovery-oriented employees*—people selected, trained, empowered, rewarded, and led in a manner that encourages and inspires them to listen empathetically and respond positively to customers with real—or imagined—woes.

As a manager you have responsibility for the former; as a leader you have influence over and accountability for the latter.

As a leader, you have a significant recovery management toolbox at your disposal—scientifically reliable selection techniques, training and coaching interventions, reward and recognition tactics, and your own skill at supporting and inspiring those you lead.

As important as these are, the most potentially powerful is you: You as a role model of service sensitivity in action, exhibiting the attitudes and behaviors that become a powerful influence in your employees' lives.

Middle managers and front-line supervisors often underestimate the influence they have in organizations, the extent to which what they say and do is closely watched and emulated by front-line workers. But looks can be deceiving.

The people who think of you as "the boss" are more than a little swayed by your actions. Like it or not, you are the personal role model for many of the people who report to you. How they see you deal with and talk about peers, employees, and customers tells them what the real rules of conduct are for your piece of the organization.

You cannot fool people into performing great recovery or caring about their customers. But you can lead them there by, as Ghandi said, "being the change you wish to create in the world." Your personal example of doing things right, taking time out to listen patiently to customers, respecting customers, focusing energy on the little things that say "above all, quality service" to your people, are critical parts of your leadership role. Through your day-to-day example and leadership, you set the tone and lead the way.

The People Imperatives

Job 1 as a service leader is to hire *good people*. It starts there or it does not start. *Train them carefully and extensively* so they have the knowledge and skills to perform great recovery. *Give them the necessary power and support to "close the deal"* and restore disappointed customers to a place of satisfaction.

Then, if you want repeat performances, let them know how much you value their work. *Recognize and reward their accomplishments,* sometimes individually, sometimes as a group. In particular, spotlight and celebrate the accomplishments of individuals and teams that go "one step beyond" for their customers. That sends a loud-and-clear signal to the whole group about the actions you value.

Managing the people side of recovery is a multifaceted, never-ending saga. Once found and brought on board, quality people must be kept in the fold. Satisfaction increases with every additional experienced, efficient, and familiar face (or voice) that greets your customers. That means not only orienting new employees carefully so they understand just exactly what you mean by high-quality service and top-notch recovery, it means training them fully in the knowledge and skills necessary for success, giving them challenging assignments, acknowledging the stresses of their jobs, and keeping them interested in the work of the organization. And sometimes it means paying them a bit better—in base or incentive pay, or other valued perks—than the competition is willing to do.

13

Find and Retain Good People

You start with good people, you train and motivate them, and you give them an opportunity to advance, then the organization succeeds.

—Bill Marriott, Jr.
CEO, Marriott Corporation

You know, we know, everyone who manages a customer service or retail sales unit knows it. You start with good people or you do not start at all. We also know that hiring well means being highly selective. When it comes to creating and maintaining a positive relationship with customers, hiring nobody sometimes is better than settling for the first warm body that promises to show up for 40 hours and more-or-less on time. You do not end up with satisfied, loyal customers if you do not start with quality people—the kind of people who get as big a kick out of delivering great service as customers do receiving it and who can remain calm, cool, and recovering under fire.

Ah, but there is the rub! In today's labor market, sometimes it seems that warm bodies are all that are left. As soon as you finally find a highly motivated, energetic, customer friendly employee and you get them trained, they are off working for an e-commerce start-up company at twice the pay—and with IPO options. The odds *against* finding, hiring, and retaining the right people for your company are much higher today than ever before:

The U.S. government projects that some sixteen million new jobs will be created by the year 2005, yet only fourteen million new workers will be wading into the labor pool in the same time frame.

Forty-seven percent of human resource executives polled by the American Management Association confirmed their organizations are now experiencing a scarcity of skilled workers. Fifty-five percent predict the shortage will last into the next decade.

Microsoft reports a skilled labor shortage among its Microsoft Solution Providers channel of 17,000 technical jobs in North America and 40,000 jobs worldwide. The Information Technology Association of America (ITAA) estimates the shortage at 190,000 unfilled IT jobs, not counting government and nonprofit organizations. One third of ITAA members reported they are recruiting IT workers on a full-time basis, and 68 percent say they are concerned that this skill shortage will become a barrier to growth.

The average U.S. high school graduate cannot do a three-step math problem, yet computers, statistical process control, qualitative measurement, and technical expertise are basic components of the workplace.

About 20 percent of the people who show up looking for a job cannot understand the instructions, "In case of emergency, pull handle," yet they have to be able to read, respond to, educate, and meet the rising expectations of ever more demanding customers on a minute-by-minute and day-by-day basis.

Bottom line: We are in a tight labor market—one that will get not only tighter, but progressively older, more diverse, and less interested in traditional low-pay, low-status, low-prestige, entry-level jobs. Your challenge? Find people who can do the job today, can keep learning so they can do the job tomorrow, can solve customer problems, will act on their own in unique and unusual situations, can remain poised under pressure, and can be relied on to act in the best interest of the customer without compromising the company.

Of course, once you find these paragons of service virtue, they must be willing to take the job and be able to work the hours it demands (including evenings, weekends, and the other odd times your customers think they want to be served), be prepared to accept a compensation package you can afford, be imbued with a commitment to stay with the task at hand long enough to gain the precious experience it takes to master it, and be balanced enough to do the work without burning out on the steady diet of stress and tension that so often goes with front-line service.

Oh yes, you also have to be able to find, hire, and retain people with these unique and special skills without inadvertently violating one or more of the dozen and a half laws and guidelines that protect job hunters and employees alike from unfair treatment and without giving them reason to start looking for greener pastures before the pressure-sensitive ink starts to set on their first payroll form. Good luck!

Is the effort worth making? Yes it is! Customer satisfaction is impacted when talented, productive employees leave the organization. Marriott Corporation estimates that there is a direct relationship between employee and customer turnover. They found decreasing employee turnover 10 percent decreases customer turnover 1 to 3 percent. A comparable Small Business Association study found that decreasing employee turnover 15 percent had a 25 percent impact on pretax profits.

And there are escalating direct operating costs associated with poor employee retention. *Accelerating Change Newsletter* estimates that it costs $30,000 to $50,000 to recruit and train a new employee today. Hewitt and Associates and the Saratoga Insti-

tute both estimate that the replacement cost of an employee is 1 to 2.5 times their salary. *Fast Company* magazine estimates that the "true cost" of hiring, training, and losing an employee to a competitor is at least $200,000 to $300,000.

Forty-five percent of 206 medium-to-large U.S. companies surveyed by New-York-based William M. Mercer, Inc., estimate that turnover costs $10,000 per employee who left. One fifth of the respondents put the cost at more than $30,000.

Front Line

Turnover in the quick-serve restaurant business is approximately 300 percent in some geographic areas, necessitating the closing of all but drive-through service.

As the labor market, especially the market for top-notch service people, continues to tighten, more and more managers are making the connection between satisfied customers who keep coming back and the loyal, motivated people who provide the service that brings those customers back. Increasingly, keeping good people is treated as a critical concern by the service elite— recession or boom.

At Walt Disney World, job rotation, cross-training, and the clearly observable fact that the road to management starts at the front line combine to give the controlled entertainment king a front-line turnover rate less than half the theme park industry average.

At Precision LensCrafters, the "glasses in about an hour" people, career movement opportunities, sales incentives, and a strong "in-group" corporate culture keep turnover low despite a very competitive, high-pressure retail setting.

In Embassy Suites properties, front-line people are rewarded with raises for learning new jobs through cross-training that is available to them even when nonimmediate openings are projected. This learning-and-earning incentive keeps turnover of front liners among the lowest in the industry (and provides an emergency staffing pool ready to respond at a moment's notice).

Finding the Best—For Recovery

Step one is to find people with good service potential. Step two is to make fitness for recovery part of that potential. It all begins with a special mind-set: Great service is a performing art. Hire as if you are casting a part in a play, not filling a job.

Guest service performers must be able to create a relationship with the audience. From the customer's standpoint, every performance is "live" and hence unique. It earns the best reviews when it appears genuine, perhaps even spontaneous. It should never be rigidly scripted and certainly not canned. Customer service cast members must have good person-to-person skills; their speaking, listening, chatting, and interacting styles should seem natural and friendly and appropriate to the situation—neither still and formal, not overly familiar.

Great service performers must be able to handle pressure. There are many kinds of pressure: pressure of the clock, pressure from customers, pressure from other players in the service cast, and a pressure from the desire to do a good job for both customer and company even though the two may be in conflict. Members of the customer service cast must be good at handling their own emotions, calm under fire, and not susceptible to "catching the stress virus" from upset customers. At the same time, they have to acknowledge and support their customers' upsets and problems and demonstrate a desire to help resolve the situation in the best way possible.

Great service performers must be able to learn new scripts. They have to be flexible enough to adjust to changes in the cast and conditions surrounding them, make changes in their own performance as conditions warrant, and still seem natural and knowledgeable. Customer service cast members need to be lifelong learners—curious enough to learn from the environment as well as the classroom, comfortable enough to be constantly looking for new ways to enhance their performance, confident enough to indulge the natural curiosity to ask, "why is that?" and poke around the organization to learn how things really work. Those who are comfortable with change and handle it well can be the most helpful to customers and need minimal hand holding from their managers.

To get a look at the candidate's recovery potential, screen test them from the moment they walk on "the stage" until they make their "exit." Consider the way applicants treat your secretary or the receptionist. That may be a good indication of how they will treat your customers and their coworkers if hired. Try role playing difficult customer situations with applicants or posing "what would you do if" questions based on the kinds of situations likely to occur on the job. You do not want to listen just for "right" or "wrong" answers. You can train them to use the right words later. Listen for orientation and attitude.

Paying Attention to Retention

All is not lost. You can effect retention in your service crew. And your whole organization. There are a variety of weapons to use to keep your employees coming back.

Compensation.   Money, the Pollyannas among us note, is not everything, to which the cynics promptly reply, "Okay, but it's a very close second to whatever's first." Service-distinctive organizations commonly pay above the average for their industry, using the tactic (1) to attract good people and (2) to keep them from seeking greener pastures. Federal Express package sorters start out at about double the minimum wage, and even part-timers are eligible for bonuses and profit sharing. Top sales associates in Nordstrom department stores can earn well in excess of $50,000 a year.

Special Treatment.   In lieu of money, individuality can compensate in a variety of ways. Instead of forcing everyone to fit into the same employee box, recognize that each needs and values different things. For parents with young children, for example, it may be flexibility around daycare; for parents whose children are a little older, it may be the opportunity to attend an occasional school program in the middle of the afternoon

Special Contracts and Perks.   Tie specific types of performance achievements to specific payoffs, whether monetary or symbolic. A "piece of the action" tells your people you value their efforts. Similarly, a special parking space, tickets to athletic or cultural events, enhanced discounts on the company's products and services, and other "spiffs" keep them from feeling taken for granted.

Training.   For today's knowledge workers, one of the most enlivening and enriching experiences is training that helps them do their job better. They know performance counts, that in many cases they're being judged on how well their customers say they are serving. Developing new talents or getting a refresher on old ones helps them stay on top of their game. It also communicates the organization's continuing commitment to them. In the pharmaceutical industry, for example, sales representatives for Merck & Co. receive the equivalent of paramedical training before ever calling on a customer. They then spend a week every other year at a major medical school to find out what's happening on the cutting edge of medicine.

Cross-Training.   In the old manufacturing-style hierarchy, you moved up or you moved out. Today, you move around, taking on new or changed responsibilities as customers change what they want from the business. The more hats your people can wear, the more valuable they can be to the organization: If their current specialty goes away or is deemphasized, they know and you know that they are ready and able to fill an emerging need instead of filling out an application for unemployment insurance. What is more, having people pretrained for other jobs helps you meet unexpected demands, from the need to replace someone who departs unexpectedly, to coping with the occasional (and unpredictable) overload situation, to the ability to respond quickly to new demands and opportunities.

Lateral Job Movement.   The most exciting and fulfilling job becomes stagnant and predictable over time. At Southern California Gas Co., lateral "developmental assignments" are used to challenge, reward, and motivate people who cannot move up (because so many layers of "up" have been eliminated in recent years). Give your people the opportunity to "switch hats" with someone else in the department, or the company at large, and you not only give them a chance to rise to a new challenge, but you also help them gain a new perspective on what they have been doing.

Empowerment.   According to Richard Leider, author of *Intrapreneuring*, the biggest problem today is not burnout, it is rustout. So many people in our organizations are capable of doing so much more than we have ever asked (or allowed) them to do. So let them. The more "ownership" they assume for the responsibilities built into their job, the more likely they are to stay with it, no matter (and perhaps because of) how challenging they find it.

Reward and Recognition.   It is axiomatic that what gets rewarded gets repeated. If you want people to stay and grow with you, recognize and reward them, not just for their years of service but also for their accomplishments along the way. For most people, the research shows that "just getting noticed" for a job well done is a more powerful motivator than money. It says you are paying attention to their individual (or team) performance and that you recognize how hard they are working, how much they are contributing, and how valuable they are.

Celebration.   If people do not, will not, or cannot laugh in the workplace, there is something seriously wrong in the workplace.

When it goes good, make a point of celebrating the victory and the people who made it possible. Use the managerial equivalent of a "high five" to recognize and thank everyone involved for their effort. That will send them back into the game, determined to win again and proud to be playing on a winning team.

Manage with Respect

One of the most important, but hardly acknowledged, components of employee retention is, are you ready for this, good management. A study called Industry of Choice, conducted by the National Restaurant Association and sponsored by Coca-Cola, makes the point. The researchers asked 3,000 restaurant employees to name the factors they considered when making a "stay/go" decision. Human resources policies and practices counted (pay, benefits, career potential), and person/job match (other employees, skills, work environment) were important. But so were the practices of their immediate supervisors. Six "boss" factors directly impact these restaurant employees' decision to stay put or move on to another place of employment:

- A supervisor who is fair
- A supervisor who does not embarrass or make fun of me
- A supervisor who treats others as they would like to be treated
- A supervisor I can get along with
- A supervisor who treats me like an adult
- A supervisor who is moral

If none of this strikes you as shocking or earth shaking, it should not. But, then again, how often have you seen these simple wants violated?

14

Train and Coach

Excellence is an art won by training and habituation. We are what we repeatedly do. Excellence, then, is not an act, but a habit.

—Aristotle

Training makes performance of potential. Even an employee who has worked in another area of your organization or was in customer service in another organization needs to be trained in your ways of doing things in your area. And most certainly someone hired from the outside, regardless of experience, needs to learn your approach to the job and to customers. It is particularly true of your approach to recovery.

Whether your employees are meeting face to face with customers or worrying over e-mail responses in the bowels of the organization, it is their skill and effort that make the difference between a recovery savvy organization and wishful thinking. Developing, honing, and keeping a competitive edge on your people's recovery skills makes strategic sense.

It is not surprising, then, that in "service successful" organizations, training and development of employees are seen as a never-ending process that includes formal and on-the-job training, guided experience, effective coaching, targeted performance review, and strong support for learning from the organization.

Providing more and better training for your people can and does create a big advantage in the marketplace. There is pretty good evidence that employees who receive formal job training

- Reach performance standards faster.
- Are better at customer problem solving.

- Create less waste.
- Stay with you longer.
- Are rated higher in knowledge, skill, and hustle by customers.

How Much Training?

Our Service Management Practices Inventory (SMPI™) data suggest that service successful organizations invest 20 to 40 hours a year in training and retraining front-line customer service people—year in and year out. By contrast, the also-rans in our database tend to depend on a "sit by Sally and ask questions" approach to training new employees and limit on-going training to a few hours of new systems installation and systems and product modifications annually.

Training in What?

Despite its importance as a competitive advantage, do not confuse training with mother love, chicken soup, or high-octane gasoline. It is not the case that if a little is good, a lot is better. Relevance counts as much as, maybe more than, minutes. To be effective, training should support serving customers better, working smarter, or creating better outcomes for the organization.

There are five kinds of training your customer contact employees need to do their jobs well: technical skills, interpersonal skills, product and service knowledge, customer knowledge, and recovery situations. All are critical to their success. All need to be addressed throughout each individual's career with you. Following are some tips for developing and honing those five crucial skill areas. The better these areas are covered, the better your employees are at recovery—they are the core skills that make recovery possible.

Technical Skills

- **Gadgets.** Front liners need to learn to work not only with your computer system—software as well as hardware,

plus associated devices such as modems, backup storage
systems, and network linkages—but all of your office
equipment. That includes the copier, fax, cash registers (if
you are a retailer), and the telephones. Yes, telephones.
Some of today's systems would surely baffle Alexander
Graham Bell.

> • **HINT:** Assume nothing about your people's
> knowledge of your systems. Even if they've
> worked with a similar technology, they haven't yet
> worked with your particular variation on the
> system theme. What they don't know can kill you
> with customers.

- **Paperwork.** They need to understand the purpose of
  your paper records and systems, not just which blanks to
  fill in with what letters and numbers, but what role customer histories, status, and incident reports, data integrity and privacy considerations, and forms filled-out
  by or for the customer play in your system of information
  management. Any time that paper affects the speed, reliability, and personal attention provided to customers,
  your people definitely need to know your forms and procedures cold. Even if you have a paperless environment,
  the imperative is the same—good record keeping and ac-
  cessible customer data make recovery efforts feel smooth
  and seemless to upset or just inquiring customers.

Interpersonal Skills

Hopefully, you hired your service people for their abilities
to listen, understand, communicate, and relate with customers
as well as their technical and product skills. No matter how good
their specific skills may be, the more practice, the more training,
the more knowledge, and the more experience you can give your
front-line people, the stronger their skills will become. The bur-
den need not fall on you alone. A wide variety of books, video-

tapes, audiotapes, web-based training, and low-cost seminars exists to remediate poor skills and polish competent ones toward mastery.

Product and Service Knowledge

- **Technical Aspects**. Customers expect your employees to know more about the products and services you sell than they themselves, as customers, do. That is not always the case, however, which is one of the prime reasons so many people prefer shopping by catalog or the Internet to shopping in brick-and-mortar shops these days.
- **Competitive Aspects**. Customers also expect your front liners to know something about the products and services your competitors sell. The more knowledge and factual information (as opposed to sales hype and "fluff" and " nonsense") they can give your customers, the less need your customers will feel for comparison shopping.
- **Customer Buy Points**. Do your employees know what questions customers ask most about your products and services? And how to answer them? Do they have a list or file of common complaints about your offerings and your competitors products? Training can help them think and sometimes anticipate a customer need or expectation.

Customer Knowledge

- **Customer Profiles**. Your customer-contact people in particular can never know too much about their customers, whether that involves the personal tastes of a consumer or the products and services of a business-to-business client. Your front liners should be helped to develop a "style" for asking questions about customers and should write down what they learn. Customers expect your people to "stay told."
- **Heavy Hitters**. Encourage customer-contact people to create files on each of their five best customers, with notes on what they learned about them. What common elements do they notice that are missing from other cus-

tomers? Would nurturing those traits build business as well as customer loyalty?

Recovery Situations

Weather grounds flights, power surges damage hardware, and acts of nature keep deliveries in the truck. Come Christmas time, stock runs low. Predictable, generally avoidable situations. Hotels overbook, airlines oversell, and car rental companies overpromise as well—all in anticipation of no-shows and last-minute cancellations. Sometimes, not often, but sometimes, we, the customer, cross them up and keep our commitments. That also can be anticipated. Training employees to recover from the most frequent, easily anticipated, and snafu problems is the key to making planned recovery work for your organization.

HINT: It is very tempting to go from predicable situations to predictable solutions—scripted responses. Don't go there! Scripted responses have two inherent problems:

- They sound canned and inauthentic.
- Most customers don't know their lines very well.

It is better, although admittedly more work, to give employees general guidelines and lots of practice. Specifically, they should be practicing the most likely to occur recovery situations your business encounters, and the cells of the CORDs matrix you developed following the description in Chapter 9.

Making Training Stick

In some organizations, training of new employees is done by someone other than their manager and someplace other than on your unit. That does not absolve you of your responsibility to ensure that the training actually makes a difference in their ability to serve customers and perform effective recovery.

Here are three things you can do to make sure the people you send off to training get the most out of the experience.

1. **Make training a highly visible event.** Create a little hoopla. Whether the training will be attended by three or one hundred, make sure that everyone knows it is important to you and the organization. Hold a short meeting. Tell everyone who is going off to training and why. Explain what will happen when they return and how everyone will benefit.

2. **Hold a pretraining "heart-to-heart" expectations talk.** Sit down—one at a time—with the employees who are going and

discuss your expectations of the training and of their participation. Specifically, discuss

- What the training will cover
- Why the individual employee is going
- Why the training is important to the organization
- Your assessment of the employee's strengths and weaknesses as they relate to the content and objectives of the training
- How you will help them apply the new skill or knowledge when they return from training

If participants are going to be expected to share their observations with others on their return, that should be made clear and precise details discussed. "When you come back, I'd like you to do a 10-minute recap of the high points at the Thursday staff meeting" is a very different expectation than, "When you come back, I'd like you to present a 2-day training program for the rest of us."

3. **Assign pretraining homework**. The last thing an employee scurrying to make plans for a 2- or 3-day absence from the job needs is homework. Just the same, preparatory readings, data gathering, worksheet preparation, and other training-related tasks can prime and focus the employee for the experience to come.

- Will the program be about dealing with unhappy customers? Ask the person going off to training to gather worst customer or biggest customer problems from coworkers.
- Is it a course on team problem solving? Have attendees interview you, other managers, or fellow employees about the greatest barriers to improving customer satisfaction with the team. (The people conducting the training can help you think through the best sort of homework to assign.)

The environment your people come back to must encourage and support their use of the new information and skills.

Here are three things you can do to help smooth the transition from classroom to real-world performance.

1. **Debrief people when they return**. It may seem as if we are recommending a lot of chatting. We are. Letting people talk about the new ideas, approaches, and skills they have been exposed to helps the transfer to the workplace while reinforcing the value you put on the new insights they have gained.

The discussion should be more than a friendly chat, however. It should be fairly detailed, and questions such as, "How do you think we can use that here?" should play a big part. Let your people show you that they have indeed come back with something new and useful. Be lavish in your praise of the new learning and ideas and of the effort the employee has put forth.

2. **Hold a skill drill or practice session for the newly trained**. We learn best by doing, but actual skill practice may be at a minimum in a training program because of the number of participants, the style of the presenter, or the inability to address specific concerns in a general session. If it is important to turn the new learning into strong habits of performance, then the sooner the effort starts, the better.

3. **Catch somebody doing something new and thank 'em for trying**. Making a new behavior an active part of an employee's skill vocabulary takes time and practice. It also takes feedback and encouragement. Particularly from you. Be sure you set goals for the use of the new recovery skill, "I expect to hear you using those new techniques with all your tough customers by the end of the month." Then follow through positively, with interest and encouragement, not officiously, with a stopwatch and a clipboard, "That sounded great, Lee. Keep trying those different techniques and I'm sure that by the end of the month you'll be handling all the tough ones without a worry."

Your Role as Coach

The similarities between service managers in business and coaches in athletics and the arts are many—and worth exploring as you try to give yourself a frame of reference for your managerial actions and responsibilities. Like a coach,

- **You instill fundamentals.** Your people have to know how to play their particular roles or positions. What to do, and when, and how. What to say, and why. Where to be when the customer feeds them a cue or throws them a curve. And just as great actors and athletes know the necessity of constant practice, of "getting in the reps" (repetitions) that help them master the part they are called on to play, you have to keep your people focusing on task and constantly honing their skills.
- **You build teamwork**. The second baseman is one of nine players on the baseball field. The violinist sitting first chair is just one player in the orchestra. No matter how individually talented they may be, the overall success of the production, be it the playing of a baseball game or a Beethoven symphony, is judged by how well everyone plays together. You position your players. You have to make sure they know how their role interlocks with others on the service team. You have to keep them focused on both their individual performance and the overall success of the group and keep the group working together in harmony in competitive conditions that challenge each in different ways.
- **You evaluate and adjust**. Every team, every individual performer, starts with a "game plan." But typically the plan can only prepare; it cannot control play from start to finish. There are other variables, often outside anyone's control, that have to be taken into account in the midst of the performance. Like a coach, a service manager has to know how to reposition players, change the script, react to immediate needs, and anticipate circumstances that may be encountered in the next quarter or the next act.
- **You reinforce and motivate.** The coach's role is to plan and prepare, react and adjust, correct problems without destroying the player's self-confidence, and praise good efforts without giving the recipient of the "well dones" a swelled head. You cannot play favorites and build a united team. You cannot preach sacrifice and dedication

and then go put your feet up while your people give everything they've got. Your words and actions set the tone for theirs.

- **You're on the sidelines**. When the manager walks onto the playing field in most sports, play promptly stops. It does not continue until the coach has returned to the dugout, or the bench, or the wings. Just as you cannot direct the play from the balcony or run the game from the locker room, you have to position yourself as close as you can to the action so you can support your players without either getting in their way or being so far removed from them that you do not know what they need from you.

15

Involve and Empower:

The Healing Magic of "Responsible Freedom"

Sooner or later you have to trust your people.

—James Barksdale
CEO, Netscape

Say the word "empowerment" to a group of supervisors or managers, and you are likely to see hair collectively raising on necks, hives beginning to form, and even a few hands reflexively covering wallets. Empowerment conjures images of front-line associates "giving away the store" to overpampered or conniving customers and of said leaders ceding precious control to those who are ill equipped to make such weighty decisions.

Empowerment—to risk a hackneyed expression—tends to mean different things to different people and to be interpreted differently depending on organizational culture. Ask for a clear definition, and you will get a wide range of answers. Yet most managers have the uncomfortable feeling empowering front-line employees is something they are "supposed to" be doing—whatever it is.

Take for instance Joe, a tough and crusty ex-union buster of our acquaintance who learned his managerial skills in the bowels of a mean, dirty, survival-of-the-fittest textile mill. Joe never smiled when he could smirk. Many an employee missed the pleasure of his morning meal worrying about an upcoming afternoon meeting with Joe.

One day Joe called a meeting to announce that the company was shifting to a participative management philosophy. Now, the idea of Joe suddenly becoming an emancipating empowerer was as likely as Donald Trump deciding to wear a $100 suit. But, if nothing else, Joe was a loyal team player, and his declaration piqued employees' interest. That is, until Joe closed the brief meeting with one final comment, "Our division will have participative management. And you will participate, by God, or I'll fire your butts!"

True empowerment is about giving employees the freedom to act both creatively and responsibly to meet customer's recovery needs. It is *not* about marching orders.

How Empowerment Fuels Recovery

Nothing sets an unhappy customer's blood boiling faster than hearing a front-line associate say, "I'll have to check with my manager." This handoff signals many things—most of them bad. It says the organization has so little regard for its customer-contact people that managers are unwilling to give them the power to make customers happy. It implies the customer will suddenly be dependent on an out-of-sight employee—not a direct eyewitness—to assess the situation based on information passed along from another source. To the customer, the transfer of problem-solving responsibility can feel demeaning, inefficient, and unfair.

Memorable service recovery—the kind that gets customers spreading the gospel—cannot happen without empowered front-line employees at the wheel. Organizations that impose on front liners a weighty list of checks and balances in routine recovery scenarios increasingly suffer by comparison. The customer who just had an American Express phone rep make a quick exception or the waiter at the local restaurant comp a dessert because of slow service is not thrilled to find you have handcuffed your people when it comes to solving customer problems. Whether dealing with sales, service, or a receptionist, today's customers do not want to put up with the hassles of pass-alongs when many of their problems could be "closed" on first contact.

Getting employees to "pick up" such power once handed to them is another issue, of course. As much as they may dream of calling more of the shots, the reality is when push hits shove, many of your people would rather someone simply tell them what to do rather than finding answers themselves to often ambiguous recovery dilemmas. Organizations today also are asking associates to do more with less and without the past promise of taking care of them come hell or high water, "In exchange for your commitment and above-and-beyond dedication, we will guarantee you a lifetime job." Those days are long in the rear-view mirror.

So how can an organization get passionate commitment without a reciprocal promise of security? The secret may lie in creating environments where leaders treat followers more like partners than subordinates. Position-based power management—the "because I said so!" type—is fast becoming the last resort of the inept. New "partner-leaders" focus less on sovereignty and more on support. Controlling takes a back seat to coaching. What does this partner-leader look like in action? How do they carry out their "in charge" position without power being the medium of exchange? Following are four common roadblocks to front-line associates "picking up their power" and solving customer problems on first contact and a few ways you, operating as partner-leader, can help them overcome each.

Simply stated, empowerment is giving the people closest to a problem, challenge, or need the authority to make judgments on the resolution of the issue. Empowerment does not mean unlimited license or "just do whatever you need to do." A better definition of empowerment is "responsible freedom."

Empowerment means helping your customer contact people balance freedom to go the extra mile for the customer with responsibility to the organization. Smart managers hire and train people who know how to simultaneously care for the customer *and* the organization, to find the middle ground that protects both sides' interests. Ignoring one side of the equation means trouble. If associates take care of the customer but discount the organization's financial well-being, the bottom line suffers. If they take care of the organization and short-sheet the customer, the result is largely the same.

Think of your job as a liberator, the one who removes obstacles and unnecessary shackles that keep your associates from acting with "responsible freedom."

Four Obstacles to an Empowered Workforce

Lack of Purpose

Front-line employees work harder and smarter when they feel they have an important part to play in carrying out a compelling mission. They also make more responsible decisions on behalf of the organization and the customer. "Vision without action is daydreaming," said the philosopher, "but action without vision is just random activity."

People will act with power if they see a greater purpose in their work than simply the day-to-day task. For front-line associates to act with extraordinary zeal or follow-through, they must believe it is their purpose to "make a customer happy" or to "make the service process work like it is supposed to." Purpose is the "Oh, so that's why I'm here!" explanation that energizes and motivates on days when it would be far easier to hit the snooze button and call in sick, or to do the ordinary when the situation calls for extraordinary.

Even after all these years, Federal Express chairman Fred Smith regularly reminds his associates of the FedEx mission, "We aren't just 'delivering stuff by 10:30 A.M.' We transport some of the most precious cargo in the world—an organ for a vital transplant, a gift for a special ceremony, a factory part whose late delivery may hold up a major enterprise."

How can you instill a sense of purpose in your people?

- Talk about your organization or unit's mission or vision often. Focus on what you want the organization to "be," not just what you want it to "do."
- When communicating performance expectations, describe the "whys"—why it will pay for the organization, for the customer, and for associates personally to fix service breakdowns—as well as the "whats" and "whens."
- Recognize corporate heroes by "telling their stories"—the details of their special accomplishments that become examples for others to follow.
- Walk the talk. Make sure your actions are consistent with the organizational mission or purpose. Where do you spend your time? What do you show excitement about? What do you show concern about? Remember, associates do not watch your mouth, they watch your moves. If you are not showing great concern for solving customer problems, you can expect your people to follow suit.
- Measure your mission. Measuring your customers' perception of how well you are doing at delivering on the implicit and explicit promises you make in your vision/mission statement clearly marks out as important what otherwise can be cynically mistaken for corporate "eyewash."

Lack of Protection

The quickest way for employees to learn whether they are "really" empowered or not is to make a visible mistake. If the error is met with rebuke and punishment, it sends quite a different message than if a manager sees error as an opportunity for learning or improved problem solving.

Without limited risk taking, there is no learning, no creativity, and, consequently, no motivation. With risks, there are occasional honest mistakes. It is far easier to gently rein in an overzealous, go-the-extra-mile associate than it is to find one with that enthusiasm in the first place. Even if it causes you some sleepless nights or Maalox days thinking of associates "out there on the high wire" making the moves necessary to fix broken customers, it is your job as supervisor to support and encourage associates so they can go out there and try it again, each time with better results.

What can you do to help associates feel they're "protected" and to build their confidence to take measured risks and trust their own judgment?

- Examine your management philosophies and practices. Punish an infraction, and, if you are not careful, you will create a precedent. Are your associates clear on what is a "thou shalt not" and an "it would be better if you didn't"?
- Recall the last few times an associate made an honest mistake. Was your forgiveness directly spoken or just tacitly implied? If the latter, the employee may not have gotten the message, making him or her more cautious—and thus more ineffective in the face of customer problems demanding bold or decisive response—in the future.
- Are associates publicly given the benefit of the doubt? If your people were questioned by an outsider, would they say they received more "constructive coaching" or "negative critiquing"?
- How often are associates praised for gallant, smart efforts that fail to pan out as planned?
- Are associates commended for seeking assistance from others to solve customer problems, including those in superior positions?

- Clarify "red rules and blue rules." Some rules have their basis in legal, safety, ethical, and solid business issues. We call those "red rules," rules that, when broken, can cause dire consequences. Blue rules are, well, just the rest of the rules. Call them operating procedures, parameters, guidelines. The trouble is, once written down, they carry the weight of corporate "law." It is important that you, as manager/leader, make clear which rules are inviolable and which can be stretched, folded, mutilated, and, when the occasion calls for it, ignored.

Lack of Permission

Your associates need guidelines, not unlimited license. The supervisor who says, "Just do whatever you think is best," is more likely demonstrating abdication (or intense fatigue) than empowerment. But those guidelines also need some "elbow room" to enable employees to tailor responses to the unique problem and the unique customer. Customers do not want uniformity in service. Although they do seek consistency, they also want to be treated as individuals. That requires some level of front-line flexibility and permission to act within relatively elastic guidelines.

It can be dangerous to assume your people will naturally know what they are and are not allowed to do to solve customer problems or even that they will believe you the first time you say, "Yes, you can." Many people have heard their bosses say "no" throughout a lifetime of working for a living, as well as in their roles on the other side of the counter, as customers seeking solutions to problems. Empowerment is a new pair of shoes that take some breaking in.

What can you do to encourage permission?

Consider this line printed on the menus in Asheville, North Carolina-based McGuffey's Restaurants, "The answer is yes. What's the question?' Apply some variation of that thinking, and the message behind it, with your people.

- Model "responsible freedom" and measured risk taking through your actions. Where you lead by example, others will follow.

- Examine your reward and recognition practices. Which do you reward with greater frequency: creativity or compliance? Being adroit and resourceful, or simply parroting company policy? Who is praised or promoted in your group—and for what specific behaviors? Apply "zero-based" budgeting thinking. If you eliminated all the rules, regulations, and polices attached to your associates' roles and then added back only those that were absolutely relevant to serving customer or organizational needs, would you be writing restrictions long into the night?
- Clone your wisdom. The conundrum is that if you were making all the decisions about all the recovery situations your people encountered, customers would almost always walk away satisfied. Think about the steps and phases, the situations and incidents that taught you the "right way" to do recovery. Can telling your tale teach others to follow your lead? Can you set up graduated risk situations that stretch and grow your people a little bit at a time?

Lack of Proficiency

The capacity to find clever, resourceful, and creative solutions to customer problems is the mark of someone prepared and empowered to go beyond the traditional, the familiar, and the ordinary. Training your people to apply recovery solutions to variety of problem scenarios—not once but with regularity—provides not just competence but also wisdom. And where competence promotes confidence, wisdom fosters power.

What can you do to boost proficiency?

- Emphasize proficiency by recognizing and rewarding those in your work group whose performance clearly stands out and by using these pros as mentors and team leaders.
- Become a lifelong learner yourself. Rosabeth Kanter of Harvard University says, "Leaders are more powerful role models when they learn, than when they teach." Develop a set of powerful, true stories to tell in company orientation and training sessions of empowered associates

who have taken actions to solve problems and cement customer loyalty. These real-life anecdotes not only send powerful messages that employees are encouraged to take empowered actions, but they also show in detail how the solutions can be implemented.

- Publish successes. If you do not have an employee newsletter to publish incidents of great service and super recovery, you can fall back on the time-honored bulletin board. Most people enjoy seeing their names up in lights—in a positive way.

16

Reward and Recognize Great Recovery

In 1986, employee turnover was 220 percent. We knew we had to change. We would hire only the best, pay them to be the best, motivate the heck out of them, and make them so happy that their energy and enthusiasm just couldn't help but result in great service. In the first three months, our turnover was 39 percent in an industry that averages 250 percent.

—Keith Dunn
Founder and CEO, McGuffey's Restaurant

Recognition and recovery may seem strange bedfellows. The implication is that rewarding well-executed recovery somehow endorses errors and encourages employees to "create more mistakes" so as to ensure a kind of self-serving, Pavlovian cycle: Create mistake, fix mistake, receive scrumptious morsel from grateful manager.

Nothing could be further from the truth, of course. Effective service leaders understand the difference between affirming specific actions that bring customers back from the brink of defection and rewarding the errors, and indifferent behavior.

Although it may seem unrealistic, maybe even borderline insanity amid the daily demands of a managerial job, taking time out to recognize good recovery can be among the best uses of your time—with the highest return on investment. Spotlighting and publicly lauding acts of deft recovery not only breeds more of the same, it gives your people more of the emotional fuel needed to continue to serve customers at a high level, day in and out.

Affirmation telegraphs priority. If affirmation goes to the squeakiest budget, frugality will reign supreme. If service recovery is affirmed, employees will want to work to solve customers' problems. Stew Leonard Jr., president of Stew Leonard's Dairy Store, recalls a time he and his senior management team were in the middle of a strategic planning meeting. His father, chairman of the board, was unable to attend and called in to report that a customer had told him the grapes in one of the stores were flat. "Dad, I'm glad you called," Stew Jr. said. "We're in the middle of strategic planning. Let me put you on the speakerphone. You can give us your thoughts on our long range plan." There was a long pause. Then Stew Sr. repeated, "I said a customer told me that the grapes were flat." It was a stark reminder of priority.

The Encasing Armor of Affirmation

Affirmation fuels positive energy and grows self-esteem, and as such it is the bicarbonate to service recovery's acidic situations. It helps build a kind of bulletproof vest front-line workers "wear" when under attack from angry customers. The way people react to and cope with criticism from irate or irrational customers is anchored to self-esteem. Those with high self-esteem are far more resilient and emotionally insulated when under assault. They are better equipped to hear the worry or insecurity cloaked behind a customer's wrath. They're also better able to troubleshoot under fire. This makes regular affirmation—recognition and reward—critical to consistently strong service recovery.

A customer service representative at Dell Computer recalled with great emotion the time she was in the midst of a fire-and-brimstone phone conversation with a customer whose order had not arrived on time. "I looked up," she remembers, " and there was Michael Dell eavesdropping on my conversation. He had a smile on his face. He never spoke. He just gave me a "thumbs up" and moved through the area. My feet did not touch ground for a week."

Affirmation and group celebration also helps reduce corrosive front-line stress. Many companies hold motivational sales rallies, in large part because the gatherings and inevitable tale-swapping help salespeople whose jobs entail hearing a lot of "no"s all day blow off steam and gain the comfort of knowing they are not alone in their struggles. So it is with service employees; such celebrations can buffer them through the emotional roller coaster of dealing with quirky customer problems, exasperating questions, and the general effects of a high-pressure workplace. At American Skandia Corp., in Shelton, Connecticut, front-line service workers gather periodically to talk about their most challenging service situations and how they handled them. There are prizes for the toughest question, the cleverest answer, or the wildest request. One American Skandia manager frames it this way, "If we had a tangible product we were selling, it would be easier since some of the customer's

anger would be directed at the failed product. But we sell and service a relationship, nothing you can hold or see. That means ALL the customer's anger is usually directed at the front-line service person. And since the confrontation is over the phone, customers can be even more hostile. Taking time out to laugh, reward, and celebrate helps our service people deal with the stress of servicing customers."

The Many Faces of Reward and Recognition

The challenge, of course, is to catch your people in the act of soothing customer hurts and saving endangered relationships. As downsizing continues to send the number of direct reports per manager skyward—and as telecommuting, outside contracting, and "virtual teaming " work arrangements force more leaders to manage from a distance—it is hard to see more than a small sampling of employee behavior, and it is harder still to catch front-line employees doing anything—good, bad, or indifferent—in person. The answer is to be prepared to recognize what you see and to get creative in using other reward mechanisms, such as peer-to-peer rewards, to recognize what you cannot.

There are as many ways to reward and recognize employees and to celebrate good customer "saves" as there are creative managerial minds. Effective leaders look to affirm evidence of two actions taken by their people:

- Assertive, responsible action when a customer is left disappointed
- Preventative action or root-cause analysis that helps head off service breakdown and leads to a reduction in problem recurrence

Reward typically connotes money: bonuses, small cash awards, financial incentives, merchandise, and other tangible payoffs in lieu of cash (although often chosen and presented in terms of their cash value). Take care with incentive programs. In some environments, health care, for instance, they can be counter to the value and ethical systems of the organization.

Recognition typically is less tangible and is the nonfinancial act of calling attention to deeds that fit the goals and values of the unit or organization. Recognition might be positive verbal approval, a handwritten "thanks for going the extra mile" note from a peer or manager, or giving the recognized employee a cherished work assignment. The key difference between recognition and monetary reward is certainty. Recognition is after the fact, awarded after behavior is exhibited or results achieved. It is not "do this, get that," on a preannounced awards schedule; rather it is "we saw or heard about you doing this—thanks." In other words, recognition plans do not guarantee awards; they are either open-ended exception-based programs with broad guidelines or discretionary, manager-administered, and controlled options. Care should be taken with high-profile, public recognition. Not all employers are enamored of being singled out in front of others. Just as recovery actions need to be tailored to the situation and the individual, so also do acts of recognition.

Celebration is a public forum for reminding everyone that problem solving on behalf of the customer is important, occasionally exciting, and highly attainable. Celebrations not only give employees a dose of public recognition and bring to light behaviors for others to follow, they help nourish group spirit. They give people a short but important change of pace from the daily pressures of serving customers, help build up an emotional reservoir for coming recovery challenges, and affirm for people they are an important part of something that really matters. Examples include pizza parties, special lunches or off-site events, banquets or the like where the focus is celebrating good service performance. To maximize the business impact from celebration, pay attention to the three "Ws" and one "H": **When** you celebrate, **Why** you celebrate, with **Whom** you celebrate, and **How** you celebrate.

There are high-profile as well as low-profile recognition and reward programs. Examples of high profile include Chase Manhattan's Corp.'s "Service Star" program featuring lapel pins, plaques, cash awards, and public recognition—much of it given

The Anatomy of Celebration

WHEN	WHY
• Marking a transition • End of project/effort • Meeting an important goal • Completing a big event	• Motivational • Modeling • Prioritizing • Stress reducing

WHO	HOW
• Led by the leader • Many, not a few • All who contribute • Important guests	• Fun, upbeat, positive • Symbols, stories, heroes • Public • Rewarding and recognizing

peer to peer—for service performance that includes good recovery; Federal Express's "Bravo Zulu"; and American Express's "Great Performers" to name a few. All come complete with detailed criteria, nomination forms and processes, award review committees, and prizes and payoffs everyone can strive for.

The only caution here: Make sure your recognition spotlight does not put employees on the spot. Some do not like the glare of public attention; respect those wishes before you force them to stand up and take a bow.

Lower-profile programs include Operations Management International's "Tag You Win" that gives a certificate in addition to "Quality Bucks" good for company merchandise, movie tickets, gift certificates, and more for customer service excellence; at Citicorp Retail Service in Denver, good suggestions for new or better ways to serve customers warrant "Bright Ideas" coffee mugs or similar keepsakes. The employee who submits the month's best idea wins a circulating trophy—a 3-foot-high light bulb.

Other companies give free video rentals, tickets to musical, sporting, or cultural events, time off with pay, or post laudatory customer letters on bulletin boards. They give recognized employees special assignments, and much more.

The bottom line: Small, lower-cost rewards can be as effective as big ones if given in the right way.

The biggest bang for the buck often comes from the simplest and most authentically delivered rewards. As managers, it can be terribly easy to lose sight of the power of a sincere "You did a great job—thanks." Yet anyone who has been recognized with such verbal affirmation or with a handwritten note or e-mail saying simply, "I appreciate the extra effort you expended solving the customer's problem," from a manager or peer they respect knows how powerful and long lasting this most informal of recognition tactics can be. At Great Plains Software in Fargo, North Dakota, employees regularly reward each other for good service performance with formal cards that say, "You Put the Great in Great Plains" across the top, with space for personal comments below. It is not at all unusual for employees to keep their cards for years after the recognized acts.

Ask yourself these questions to gauge your own rewarding and recognizing behavior:

1. Have you held a team or unit performance celebration in the last 3 months?

2. Do you preplan even a few recognition and reward events for your service team?

3. Can you add inexpensive but meaningful reward and recognition events to the way you "do business"" on your team? Have you considered creating peer-to-peer service award programs, which often are seen as more credible than manager-to-employee awards and allow you to "extend your reach" by rewarding exemplary behavior you could never hope to witness yourself?

4. In today's multiple-balls-in-the air, everybody-wants-a piece-of-you working world, it can be downright impossible to find a place for reward, recognition, or celebration on your daily, weekly, or even monthly to-do lists. But we suggest you take a hard look at those lists to see what might be bumped in favor of more regular affirmation and pats on the back for your staff. You will likely find the tradeoff a good one—for the feeling it gives you, the motivational boost it gives your people, and the bottom-line bump it gives your organization in terms of better-served and more loyal customers.

17

Support and Inspire Performance and Persistence

> Perfection is not attainable. But if we chase per-
> fection, we can catch excellence.
>
> —Vince Lombardi
> *Football coaching legend, Green Bay Packers*

We love to hear recovery stories of service pros who snatched victory from the jaws of defeat, who through their nimble thinking, sympathetic bearing, and top-notch training turned customer anger into awe, enhancing their company's bottom line along the way. Sometimes these stories are laced with clever, out of the box solutions; more often they are about simple, caring efforts to see service mishaps from the customer's eyes and take the one extra step, or make the one extra call, to right a wrong.

Front-line service workers usually are the focus and heroic characters of these stories. But behind the "service magician" almost always is a backstage hand—a boss—with the capacity to facilitate and inspire such greatness. Who are these leaders that unleash and enable such effort and caring? What do they do that encourages such front-line boldness, and the day in, day out desire to fix customer problems both daunting and pedestrian? Do they simply hire go-getters and then get out of the way, or are there some explicit and well-defined leadership behaviors that pave the way to heroism?

We examined these questions in two ways. First, data from our Service Management Practices Inventory (SMPI) point to some distinct differences between "great" service managers and the also-rans. The SMPI is a (one hundred item) instrument that has been administered to 80,000 managers in 400 companies around the globe. Second, we asked people in the many organizations we have consulted to or worked with to point us to the best "service recovery practitioner" in the company, and then we asked questions about that person's supervisor.

Combining our quantitative and anecdotal data, we arrived at a revealing anatomy of inspiration.

Inspirational Leaders Are Authentic

- "He is the most jarringly open manager I've ever encountered," says executive vice president Colleen Barrett of her boss Herb Kelleher, chairman of Southwest Airlines.
- "When Rich Teerlink speaks to Harley-Davidson dealers," comments Bill Bailey about his now retired CEO, "No one doubts he is telling the truth, the whole truth, and nothing but the truth."

What do Kelleher and Teerlink have in common? They are confident enough to be real and to understand that even the least insightful or lowest ranking of their employees usually can see through pretense. Realness creates safety in relationships. The flip side of authenticity—posturing, conning, manipulating, withholding—creates an environment of caution, uncertainty, and protection, which are conditions that run counter to the limited risk taking often necessary to solve customer problems.

Safety is an important context for effective service recovery. Without some sense of a managerial safety net—an understanding there will not be punitive action if front liners take actions on the customer's behalf that a manager later disapproves of—your front-line people are reluctant to pursue out-of-the-ordinary solutions to turn customer disdain into delight and to take the small risks that regularly cement customer loyalty. Without a

CBUSH

sense of security, front liners do not go the extra mile; they only go the minimum distance needed to keep their jobs and to steer clear of management's potential wrath.

Authenticity is important in another crucial way. "Real" managers are not prone to saying one thing and doing another; they are amazingly congruent. Their language, behavior, and goals tend to be consistent from day to day, so their people do not have to waste precious psychic energy worrying about which of the manager's many personalities—or ever-shifting performance goals—will show up that day. Only through walking the talk do leaders gain the kind of credibility and respect that make their people want to break down walls to help aggrieved customers.

Of course, authenticity is not achieved overnight. Margery Williams captured the evolution well in her famous children's book, *The Velveteen Rabbit*. "Real isn't how you are made," said the Skin Horse." It's a thing that happens to you...It doesn't happen all at once, you become. It takes a long time. That's why it doesn't often happen to people who break easily, or have sharp edges, or who have to be carefully kept."

Inspirational Leaders Are Passionate

"There is an energy field between humans," wrote *Love and Will* author Rollo May. "And when a person reaches out in passion, it's usually met with an answering passion." Passionate connections provoke passionate responses. When leaders are passionate with their people, it triggers a passionate response in return. And leadership is fundamentally about influencing. People may be instructed by reason, but they are inspired by passion.

Ask twenty people to name the greatest leaders of all time, and you might get a few hard-nosed military generals, political caretakers, or technocrats back in response. But the list will likely be dominated by those who stirred their followers with fire rather than those who tried to influence or persuade through reason. Winston Churchill, Martin Luther King, JFK, Mother Teresa, and Gandhi were not famous for their rationalism, although they certainly had that trait, nor is Southwest Airlines chairman Herb Kelleher, Bruce Nordstrom, the late Sam Walton, or the late J. Willard Marriott, Sr. True leaders' invitations to action are embossed on their own yearnings to express their "cause" to others in ways that encourages them to join.

Service people need passionate connections, a reason to see their work as a higher calling, not just an assembly-line processing of customer requests or problems. Leaders who come soaring from the heart awaken passion in others. Passionate connections are laced with authenticity, realness, and openness. As such, they melt away the adversarial distance not only between boss and subordinate, but between front-line worker and customer. As one manager eloquently told us, "Words are tools for the head and the head always doubts; feelings are tools for the heart and the heart believes."

In times of service breakdown, customer wrath can be dissipated by a passionate connection, a feeling the service provider truly cares about a positive outcome for the customer. When you role model that passion for your people, odds increase that they will pick up the baton and show some of the same enthusiasm on the all-important front lines.

Inspirational Leaders Are "Courageously Supportive"

Late one evening in the lobby of the J.W. Marriott Hotel in Washington, D.C., a highly irritated guest was berating a front-desk clerk. The guest's profanity and personal attacks were in stark contrast to the elegant décor and serene setting. From out of nowhere, a short, middle-aged man emerged, walked straight to the angry guest, and said, "Sir, I need you to leave my hotel immediately." Sensing he was dealing with more than just a garden-variety manager, the guest quickly took the cue. More important, the front-desk clerk was noticeably relieved—and visibly inspired.

Inspirational leaders like Bill Marriott are willing to go to the mat for their beliefs and values. They look fear in the face and put their reputations on the line for what is important. This does not mean they are foolhardy dare devils. A leader who goes down in flames over an untenable situation is of no use in future battles. Although these leaders never back away from a conflict of principle, they do pick their scrimmages based on what actions will provide the best modeling and send the strongest messages.

These leaders also understand how downright challenging the job of customer contact can be. When their people come to them complaining of customer abuse, conniving behavior, or outrageous demands, they know they have an ally in the leader, someone who sets high performance standards and hears out both sides but who also clearly "has their back." Knowing they have that level of support is crucial not only to taking the limited risks necessary to good recovery but in mustering the enthusiasm to go face to face or phone to phone in the trenches with customers for yet another long day.

Boldness is another defining trait of these leaders. The philosopher Goethe captured the attribute thusly, "Whatever you can do, or dream you can, begin in boldness. Boldness has genius, power, and magic in it. Until one is committed, there is hesitancy, the chance to draw back, always ineffectiveness. The moment one definitely commits oneself, then Providence moves,

too. All sorts of things occur to help one that would never otherwise have occurred."

Boldness is the life blood of service recovery. It requires
boldness to put yourself in the firing line of customers who have
just unloaded both barrels on one of your people and who have
paused only briefly to reload. It takes boldness to concoct and
deliver a recovery response that is beyond the scope of "organi-
zationally approved" guidelines to satisfy a particularly unique
customer. It takes boldness to go back to an aggrieved customer
following a failed recovery attempt to make things right the second or third time, with the customer's hostility still smoldering
and ready to reignite on your smallest misstep or wrong choice
of words.

Inspirational Leaders Are Results Oriented

Authenticity, passion, and courage are admittedly "soft"
concepts, difficult to attach a dollar value to. There is nothing
soft about great recovery, however. Inspirational leaders are
fans of what works, of what keeps customers content and filling
their organization's till rather than the competition's. They are
not interested in recovery simply as a social etiquette ploy for
service faux paus.

Results oriented means asking the tough questions—oft
times repeatedly—to unravel the cause of service breakdown
and "fix the leak" at its source. Great recovery ceases to be great
if you are forced to do it repeatedly for the same problem. Results oriented means implementing the tools and techniques that
make service recovery effective, efficient, and consistent. It also
means taking a turn at the helm from time to time to get a true
picture of stormy customer encounters and the workaday challenges faced by employees in the trenches. Herb Kelleher occasionally loads baggage for Southwest on busy travel days at Dallas' Love Field. Rich Teerlink visits motorcycle dealerships,
riding his own Harley-Davidson. Such leaders are quick to personally demonstrate what is really important.

"Attention is all there is," writes management consultant
Tom Peters. "You are as good as—or as bad as—your calendar."

Results oriented means sending unmistakable messages to your front-line people by consistently putting visible energy on matters of substance and not matters of form, and by letting them know where customers rank on the organizational totem pole. It suggests working *with* employees to help support them in doing the "right things right"—those that fix unhappy customers and promote enduring customer loyalty.

Front-line workers can only be the balm to customers' service wounds with credible, courageous, and passionate support at their backs. Next time you find your people struggling to make things right for upset customers, broaden your fact-finding inquiry beyond their skills, knowledge, and attitudes to what you yourself are doing to grease the skids for great recovery along the firing lines.

Part Five

The Service Recovery Toolkit

It is easy to smile when everything's fine and life flows along like a song. But, the man worthwhile is the man with a smile when everything goes dead wrong.

—Old childhood poem

Customer service professionals need every edge they can get, especially when service recovery is the matter at hand. This section is packed with all the aids, tips, tricks, and helpful hints we have assembled. Read them, tuck them away, and have them available when your people need them. We know they will come in handy—sooner or later.

18

A Rage Apart:

Recovery and the Customer from Hell®

There are no "bad" customers; some are just harder to please than others."

—Someone who never waited on a customer in his or her life

Customers at one time or another can all fall into bad moods, get cranky or highly irritable, or even fly off the handle a bit. Your front-line folks may catch them on the heels of their car's transmission breaking down, a job being lost, a bank loan denied, a son being summoned into the principal's office, or simply amid the cumulative effect of having kept multiple work-and-family plates spinning in the air all day.

But out there looms a whole different species of customer, one whose irritating, irrational, or irksome antics are not usually a function of situation but rather of DNA, entrenched world view, and/or a perpetual victim state of mind—those we call Customers from Hell.® Customers from Hell belittle, demand, threaten to get physical, throw tantrums, spew profanities, lie, and basically "go postal" on customer-contact people on a regular basis. Picture "road rage" transferred to a bank lobby, airline check-in counter, or a call center 800 line, and you get a picture of this rogues' gallery of egocentric, hysterical, free-loading, or foul-mouthed characters.

The Customer from Hell (CFH) requires a particularly well-fortified and Teflon-coated recovery response; a CFH is specially trained to probe for and exploit weaknesses in your service recovery flanks. Your people need to be at least as well trained and armed to deal with the CFH.[1]

Four Tactics for Dousing the Flames

Our research suggests four tactics for calming the "service rage" brought forth by Customers from Hell spawn themselves:

1. **See no evil, hear no evil.** Customers from Hell can only reach their true offensive and confidence-rattling potential when service providers act as enablers. These customers count on being able to goad your people into joining their game, because if the customer service representative loses control, the CFH wins. When your associates get triggered and erupt, the CFH can come back with a näive-sounding, "I was only trying to solve my problem when that service representative just lost it all over me."

There will be times when customers get particularly hysterical that you have to let them vent and wind down a bit—accepting their feelings of anger rather than trying to convince them from the get-go there is no reason for such reactions—before you can engage them in rational conversation. However, if the temper tantrums and inciting actions persist, ignoring them sends a strong message, "Rage, cuss, and go ballistic all you want. I am not intimidated nor will I join in the escalation." Demonstrating that level of calm and unflappability gives you

---

1. A school of thought holds that a manager should never admit, at least in the presence of another front liner, that there is any such thing as a customer who is a royal pain in the butt. Calling them difficult might be okay, but "SOB" or "CFH" probably is not. The thinking goes that if front liners call them out as such, they also will feel free to give Customers from Hell the treatment they deserve rather than coddling them so money keeps flowing into the till. We refute the argument on two grounds: (1) Most front liners are not in the kind of deep denial that leads them to believe Customers from Hell do not walk the earth. (2) Many have come face to face or phone to phone with living, breathing, flesh-and-blood versions, at least on a few occasions.

the upper hand and quickly draws down the CFH's oxygen supply.

Be like Teflon to the customer's sticky anger or upset, and let the rage wash over you. Customers from Hell rarely are mad at you personally; it is the situation they despise. And if you start thinking of your customers as jerks or idiots, it will not be long before you are treating them as badly as they treat you.

One reminder: Do not use your company's service policies or procedures as a shield against Customers from Hell ("Our policy says you'll have to . . .). It will simply give them something concrete to turn against you. And besides, the more egocentric of these customers expect to be exempt from such policies. Rather, say something like, "For you, I can offer," and then offer whatever your standard policy says.

2. **Surface the tension.** Surfacing the tension is a tactic to gently remind customers lost in the middle of a rant that you, too, are a living, feeling person who is simply trying to do his or her best. Try this question, "Have I personally done something to upset you? I'd like to help. Please give me a chance." This will

help draw the Customer from Hell's attention back to the problem, not to you, the person who is become the embodiment of it. It is the rare customer—yes, even that ranting CFH with a barethread connection to rational or civil behavior—who will not, even if grudgingly, give you a chance.

3. **Transfer transformation.** There will be times when you simply will not be able to help Customers from Hell. Be it incredibly foul language, highly personal attacks, or a refusal by the customer to let you help them, you will reach the end of your rope or will not be able to let the customer's bile slide off your back. Sometimes the old saw of "It's not you they're lashing out at, it's the organization" just doesn't work on a particularly bad day. Transferring the customer to a peer or supervisor at this point is not a cop-out. Rather, in any of intolerable conditions listed, it can be a shrewd, planned-out method for moving beyond the Customer from Hell's brutal behavior.

Transfers also can have another big benefit: Putting the customer on hold sometimes has a calming effect. When they are shifted to that neutral space awaiting transfer to a coworker or boss, they are, in effect, placed in an "adult time out." Transitioned into a different activity, the customer is given a chance to leave the tantrum, and nasty talk, behind and start anew.

4. **Build contractual trust.** There also will come times—few and far between we hope—when Customers from Hell actually threaten you verbally or physically, even start to push or shove when their "service rage" caroms out of control in face-to-face recovery situations.

Here is where you need to draw a line in the sand—not one that forces your customer into the freezing water of the river but one that helicopters them out of the situation and drops them on the far bank. Most customers will comply with your requests to "please stop this behavior and I'll help you, continue and I won't." But if they do not, it is imperative you follow through. You may have to repeat the comment a second time, then give the customer a moment to realize you are dead serious. This builds what psychologists call "contractual trust." In other words, you made a promise, "I'll be forced to call security if you don't stop," or "Excuse me, but I don't have to listen to that kind of language and I'm going to hang up right now," and you kept it.

"I" statements are important in these threatening situations. They clearly communicate that you need the customer to stop a certain behavior, such as pushing, grabbing, or swearing, because although others might let that behavior slide, you simply cannot accept it.

19

Winning Words and Helpful Phrases

A great comeback makes your day.

—Anonymous

"But I haven't memorized my lines," complained actor Dennis Hopper to director Francis Coppala during the making of "Apocalypse Now." "You learn your lines," advised Coppala, "so you can forget them and improvise." Hopper did learn his lines and ad libbed his way to a spectacular movie performance. The movie won the Academy Award for Best Picture; Coppala won one for Best Director.

Scripts and clever lines are not offered as service recovery cue cards. We have found that knowing a few great comeback lines can provide front-line people the confidence to "forget them and improvise" when under the gun of service anxiety. Although these are slightly tailored for specific industries, they can easily be modified and customized for your most likely recovery situations. We invite you to add to this list with the help of your employees. A couple of hints: Do not be afraid to use humor with your customers. The judiciously placed, "How in the world did that happen?" can diffuse a situation and lighten the atmosphere. It is just as important to be able to recognize those occasions when humor is absolutely not appropriate and when a serious tone is needed. Above all, remember to always treat your customer with respect. Never belittle or criticize his problem. You never know; you could very well be in his shoes tomorrow or the next day!

In Cases of Customer Error

The three examples that follow represent only a few of the possibilities of situations you might encounter with a customer who somehow is responsible for creating a problem with a product or service. Remember, customers in these situations are already feeling guilty, stupid, or desperate for your help. They need you to tell them you will do your best to help them. In many cases, you are their last hope.

The Case of the Unproofed Proof

CUSTOMER: I can't believe I didn't catch that on the proof! This is going to set us back weeks. My boss is going to hit the roof. Help!

CSR: Rita, I'm so sorry this happened. Let's figure out what we can do. First, I should be able to get the corrected brochure back on the press this afternoon. That means we should be able to have final product back for you by end of day tomorrow. We can also assist you with folding and labeling. That should help some. I can also offer you the new brochures at cost. Will that help?

Help—I've Downloaded and Can't Get Back Up!

CUSTOMER: I knew as soon as I clicked on "Start download now" that I should've backed up my files. I'm totally screwed—the hard drive has all my financial data on it from the last decade—and I just found out I'm being audited. You've gotta help me!

TECH: Whoa, Dude! I can totally relate. I can usually figure out in about 2 hours if the damage is repairable. If so, I should be able to retrieve your files in about 24 hours. If there is severe damage, I know of a guy who does this stuff all the time. He's pretty big bucks, but he can usually get the job done. Do you want to start with that? Also, if you can write down the names of your most important files, I can start looking for those first.

Web Site Woes

CUSTOMER: Um, hi. I was just on your web site ordering your special lobster dinner. When I printed out my e-mail confirmation, I realized my "1" key must stick. I think I ordered 1,111 dinners instead of just one. Can you fix my order before my Visa card explodes?

CSR: Gosh, I wish I could. Have you considered hosting a special New Year's Eve dinner for the homeless people in your community? You might also be interested in our extra large butter warmer—that's on page 42 of our catalog. I'm sorry, I couldn't resist! Of course, we can correct your order. I'm sure the people in fulfillment would've caught it as well, but let's take care of it now. Do you still have your customer order number? It should be on that same e-mail.

In Cases of Company Error

Often times when an error or mishap occurs, not one individual can be blamed, but the error is clearly the fault of the company or even a company vendor. When these situations arise, it is important to not shirk responsibility for the mistake or try and pass the blame on. Customers and clients can see right through that. Acknowledge the error, apologize for the inconvenience, and help the customer set things right—any way you can. The following examples will give you some places to start.

There Must Be Some Mistake . . . I'm George Jones, Not Georgette Jones . . .

GEORGE: I just received an invoice that indicates that I received a hysterectomy on the 24th of last month. As I'm sure you can tell from my voice, that's a physical impossibility. How long do you think it will take for me to convince you this bill is incorrect?

CSR: Mr. Jones, I'm so sorry for this inconvenience— and I want to thank you for bringing it to our attention. Let's see if we can take care of this mix-up right now. Can I get your patient number? Did you receive any kind of medical treatment on the 24th?

GEORGE: My number is 425679732. I was in on the 24th for a CAT scan and chest x-ray. The chest x-ray is on the invoice, but not the CAT scan.

CSR: Ah, that explains a lot. See, a CAT scan is #475 in the computer and a hysterectomy is #457. I guess we must have transposed the number. I'm so sorry. Mr. Jones. I'll contact data processing, record keeping, accounts receivable, and your clinic, and I'll correct any misinformation they might have. I'll also send you out a revised statement that will indicate the correction. Is there anything else I can do to ease your mind?

GEORGE: No, that will be terrific. I dreaded calling all those places myself. If you can take care of all those details, I'll be thrilled to pieces. Thank you.

Your Store Is Trying to Rip Me Off—I Thought You Were Better Than That!

CUSTOMER: I just bought this dress and the sign said it was 40 percent off, but it rang up only 25 percent off. You know, I just saw a segment about this very same thing on "Dateline." For some reason I assumed this store was above taking advantage of its customers. Obviously, I was mistaken.

CSR: Ma'am, I apologize profusely for this mix-up. I saw that same show, and I can't tell you how proud I was to be working here and not at one of those other stores. We try as hard as we can to make sure our sale prices are reflected in all our computers. Unfortunately, on rare occasions, we miss a markdown. I would be pleased to refund the difference, as well as offer you a complimentary gift wrap or perhaps a cappuccino from our coffee shop. In addition, I will personally make the appropriate change to the computer as soon as we're done talking.

In Cases of Disaster Caused by Mother Nature

One of the most stressful times for customers and service providers alike are situations when disaster happens. Customers need answers, and they need them quickly. Or they need supplies, but they have no resources. They need to know you will not desert them in their time of need. How you meet the needs of your customers in disaster situations will have tremendous impact on your ability to retain that customer.

The Water Level Is Rising, My Blood Pressure Is Rising, Please Tell Me You'll Honor Your Guarantee

CUSTOMER: I'm calling you from the eighth step in my basement and if I'm put on hold again, it will probably be the tenth step by the time you get back to me. What I need to know is, "What is the guarantee on your foundation sealer?"

CSR: Well, Sir, can you tell me what model of sealer you bought? Was it the 15-year, 25-year, or lifetime product?

CUSTOMER: Does it really matter? I think the empty can is floating by the washing machine, and it's pretty hard to get to.

CSR: Well, I would recommend you take care of your family and most precious belongings first. With our lifetime guarantee product, if applied properly—which I'm sure it was—we will handle any repairs to your foundation. If you can grab one of the empty cans for proof of purchase it would be helpful, but if you can't, after the flood, go to any builder supply store and get our toll-free number and address off the can. I don't want to bother you with that now. Give us a call, and we'll send an inspector out to evaluate the damage and get you taken care of as soon as possible. Sir, please, for now, just make sure you and your family are safe. We'll be here to help you after things have calmed down a bit.

It Was a Stormy Night . . . But I Still Want to See Tyson Bite Someone's Ear Off!

CUSTOMER: Yes, my satellite dish appears to have been struck by lightning and now my picture is all snowy. When can I have it fixed? I want to catch the fight tomorrow night.

CSR: That was quite a storm last night, wasn't it! Let me do a quick check and see if indeed that is the problem. It's also possible that the wind moved the dish a bit out of position. No, you're right, it does seem to be a power problem. I can get a repair technician out there within 24 hours. Is morning, afternoon or early evening better for you.

In Cases of Product Failure

The last type of recovery situation we will talk about are cases when the product just does not perform to customer expectations. In these cases, you may want to refer back to Chapter 15, where we talk about red versus blue rules. When you can help your customer resolve his product dilemma through an exchange, refund, or discount, it may behoove you to do so. However, be aware of manufacturer policy on product returns. Following are three more cases to get you thinking. Remember, the customer may not always be right, but he is always the customer!

The Case of the Expired Warranty

CSR: Ms. Weinbring, I've checked with my manager, and she said that because the warranty for your bread machine expired over 18 months ago, we aren't able to offer you a complimentary replacement. I can, however, offer you a 25 percent discount for a different model by the same manufacturer. I can also give you the address for the manufacturer. They may allow you to return it for repair or replacement, even though the warranty has expired.

CUSTOMER: Okay. Let me get the address. I really don't want to buy another machine if this one can be repaired. Thanks.

Oh, Brother, Get a Grip, Would You, Pez?

CUSTOMER: What is wrong with you people? How dare you sell such inferior merchandise! I demand to speak with your manager.

CSR: Sir, I'm sorry you're so upset with your Pez dispenser, but the head is supposed to go back— that's what dispenses the candy. I would be happy to refund your money if you'd like, or I'm happy to get my supervisor. I'm sure he'd be pleased to discuss your concerns.

The Case of the Unsatisfied Infomercial Customer

CUSTOMER: I got your product from your infomercial. What a crock!! It doesn't work, it arrived damaged, and I want my money back.

CSR: Ma'am, I'm sorry you were unhappy with our merchandise. As you know, we gladly offer a 30-day, no-questions-asked, money-back guarantee. We'll be glad to credit your account, as soon as we receive the merchandise. Do you have our return address?

A Baker's Dozen of Opening Lines and Helpful Phrases

It is a Homer Simpson moment. The next morning, in the shower, you finally come up with the perfect thing to say to Mrs. Murphy. But it is 20 hours too late. And by the time you are out of the shower, you forgot it anyway. The following thirteen phrases come from the lips of the hundreds of customer service representatives we studied, interviewed, and watched at work. Their use is obvious. Their effectiveness is sworn to by the seasoned pros who shared them with us.

1. "I understand your concern. What do you think would be fair?"

2. "Julie, I'm so very sorry this has happened. How can we resolve this for you?"

3. "Sir, you deserve the very best and we seem unable to provide it. Because I want you to be well served, may I suggest . . . ."

4. "Although you may not agree with my decision, I'd like to explain it so you will at least understand."

5. "Let me do some investigating on my end and call you back. Would you prefer me to call you this evening at home, or tomorrow morning?"

6. "Have I done something personally to upset you? I'd like to be part of the solution."

7. "Thank you for bringing this matter to our attention. We will address it right away."

8. "We love to hear feedback from our customers—both positive and negative. It gives us a chance to always be upgrading our service to you. Thank you for sharing your concerns with us."

9. "It is obvious that I have not been able to help you. If you don't object, I would like to let a colleague of mine attempt to better meet your needs."

10. "Unfortunately we are unable to give you a full-price refund without a receipt. I can, however, authorize a store credit for the current sale price."

11. "We see this differently, and I am going to have to put more thought to the perspective you have shared with me. It's helpful for me to understand how you see things. In the meantime, here is what I can do to solve the immediate problem."

12. "If I hear that language again, I won't be able to assist you. Unless we can find a different way to communicate, I'm going to have to hang up." (Then, keep your promise.)

13. SERVICE PERSON: Certainly Miss, what seems to be the problem?

IRATE CALLER: Let me speak to your immediate supervisor this instant!

20

Recovery on the Phone

> If I pick up a ringing phone, I accept the responsibility to ensure the caller is satisfied, no matter what the issue.
>
> —Michael Ramundo
> *President, MCR Marketing, Inc.*

Whether broken customers emerge from recovery situations with a smile on their face and spring in their step or whether they come out with jaws clenched or stomachs pitted—with mouths or fingers operating at full throttle telling friends, coworkers, or Internet chat rooms about the abysmal experience—is increasingly a function of how they are dealt with over the phone by call center representatives.

Industry experts estimate that some 60,000 to 70,000 call centers employing almost three million people currently operate today in corporate America, with that number set to grow exponentially beyond the year 2000. Because a core function of these centers is to efficiently answer customer questions and clear up myriad product or service problems, they have, in effect, become service recovery clearinghouses, ground zero for effective complaint handling.

Yet experts say if you think you are doing customers an enormous favor simply by virtue of creating such dedicated nerve centers, you may need to think again. For investments in 800 number call centers to truly pay off, the live bodies manning the phones have to solve a large percentage of customer problems on first contact, not after repeated call backs or attempts.

And that requires the right mix of high-tech computer systems and high-touch human support.

According to data from TARP, such "world-class" closure means resolving customer problems on first contact about 85 percent of the time. Industry observers usually mention American Express, Toyota, Ford, and USAA in that category.

Why is first-contact closure so important? For the simple reason that, without it, you face the double whammy of lower customer satisfaction and escalating phone expense.

In experiments TARP did at IBM and Coca-Cola, service reps there gave half the customers who called an 800 number an answer on the first call. For the other half of customers who called, the reps said, "Gee, we're going to have to investigate that," and later called them back. What TARP found is that when reps called customers back and gave essentially the same answer, there was 10 percent lower satisfaction. A "no answer" on first contact cost the organization 10 percent, but it also cost about 50 percent in additional expense, TARP found, because if the customer has to call you back or you have to call him back, it reduces the chances you are going to connect. It becomes the equivalent of three call-backs—and greater phone or even labor expense.

Research done by TARP at hundreds of other organizations supports those findings: 10 percent average higher customer satisfaction and about 50 percent reduction in cost of the transaction when closing customer problems or answering questions on first contact.

Using high tech to provide high-touch customer service pays dividends beyond individually satisfied customers, says John Goodman, who heads up TARP. The organization's data show that if you can impress customers by rapidly solving their problems over the phone, their willingness to buy other products from you is even higher than had you not had the problem—in many cases about 8 percent higher than if customers had no problem whatsoever.

Of course, high first-contact closure rates require a well-trained workforce using all the benefits of new technology. It also requires your phone reps have adequate problem-solving

authority. To wit: TARP worked with a credit card company in Canada where the average customer was worth $1,200 in gross contributions over a 3-year period. Phone reps there were empowered to spend $25 in goodwill to help satisfy unhappy customers; anything more than that required permission from the comptroller's office. That limited empowerment piqued Goodman's interest. He asked the comptroller, "Let me get this straight. Reps need no permission for the $25, but what if they refuse a customer's request in some way? In other words, can they say 'no' to a customer without asking the comptroller?" The comptroller responded that reps can turn down customer requests at any time. But pondering the question got the comptroller's wheels turning. Before long, Goodman says, reps at the company were empowered to spend up to $200, no questions asked, in goodwill to right customer problems, but if they wanted to give a flat-out "no" to the customer, they had to seek permission.

Even the best-trained and highly empowered call center reps face challenges in performing good day-to-day service recovery, of course. Call center employees tend to be among the lowest paid and most highly pressured of an organization's staff —not to mention the omnipresent, Big Brother-ish "this call may be monitored to assure quality performance." Many also are forced to serve two conflicting masters: call efficiency and service quality. On the one hand, they are told to do everything possible to satisfy the customer and resolve their complaints; on the other hand, they are told to do it in 3 minutes, then move quickly on to the next call.

Call center reps cannot adequately resolve customer problems if there is not a good balance between the two metrics. Some TARP data actually show that spending more time with customers in the short run can save costs in the long term.

TARP studied fifty of the largest MasterCard call centers in North America to identify those that were "world class"—centers with the most loyal customers who had the highest rates of satisfaction. The data showed that average talk time in these centers was 60 to 80 seconds longer per call than in other centers. At first, TARP researchers viewed that as bad news, because it implied it was more expensive to have highly satisfied customers. But another look at the data showed that each of those accounts required fewer calls per year. In fact, Goodman says, the extra minute or so on the phone made it 20 percent cheaper to service those accounts because they made many fewer calls. By spending the extra time up front, the centers would not receive that second, third, or fourth call.

Goodman's biggest complaint with call centers? Most spend 97 percent of their time responding to the individual customer but less than 2 percent exploring the root causes of complaint calls.

Making the Best Use of New Technologies

In general, Goodman says voice response systems are not appropriate for transactions requiring time-sensitive data, interactions that might provoke unpleasant customer reactions, or complex technical assistance issues. They are ideal, however, for dealing with customer calls that ask for basic, oft-repeated information. That frees your reps for more complex, value-adding transactions, such as service recovery situations.

A 1997 TARP study examined use of technology in "best-in-class" call centers, defined as those reporting "customer satisfaction with contact experience" of more than 85 percent. A few highlights:

- **Exemplars deftly mix high touch with high tech.** Best-in-class call centers design their technology with customer needs, not just efficiency standards, in mind. For instance, when implementing interactive voice response systems, these exemplars limit the number of menu options, often to four; strive for clear and pointed scripting; engage "human factor" experts in design; and develop effective educational approaches for customers faced with the technology for the first time.
- **They make full use of technology to enhance efficiency.** Not only do the exemplars report being aggressive users of technology, more use it to its fullest. Some 54 percent of best-in-class centers use automated case tracking software for unresolved customer issues, for example, while only 33 percent of other call centers do.
- **Best-in-class respondents provide their customer service representatives with a broader array of online tools** with which to quickly serve customers—customer contact histories, customer information files, credit billing information, internal functions directories, and the like—than other less effective call centers.

Working on the assumption you *do* want unhappy customers to complain—those taking time to complain at least offer you the chance to heal their wounds, whereas those with negative experiences who do not complain usually just drift away into the ethers and on to the competition—your voice response systems should ensure customers do not get frustrated navigating menus and abandon ship before they have a chance to lodge a complaint. TARP's research finds that customers will tolerate four options; anything beyond that and they say, "To heck with it! Get a carbon-based life form in here, ASAP."

Some Tips for Good Phone Recovery

Service recovery over the phone does hold advantages over the face-to-face variety. The physical separation creates a level of detachment that often makes it easier to deal with conflict or inflammatory situations. It can be much more difficult to cope with physically intimidating or verbally abusive customers in person. Nonetheless, recovering via phone has challenges as well. Some customers arrive angry. Other customers have their anger ignited during the phone call and, without the benefit of visual cues, it is sometimes hard for phone reps to see it coming.

Here are a few ideas for handling recovery situations over the phone. For more tips on dealing with irate customers, see Chapter 18 on "Customers From Hell."

- **Frame probing, confirming, and background questions correctly.** Sometimes unhappy customers do not know what you need to know until you tell them, and you will need to ask questions to unearth that information or probe deeper to find the true cause of problems. Questions that confirm also help verify you have correctly understood the customer's problem; questions seeking background help direct customers to the right person in the organization to help them.

When asking background questions, angry customers often become incensed when you ask for things such as a social security number or mother's maiden name. In that case, you may need to just listen for awhile and take notes, before asking the questions that log you into the customer's account. Let the customer vent a bit, then ask, "I appreciate your concern, Mr. Jones. If you can help me with a bit more information, I'll get you connected to the right person right away." Or, "Mr. Jones, if you give me a little more information, I'll pull up your records and see what we can figure out."

With probing-type questions—"Could you tell me more about that?" or "What do you need to happen now?"—remember you are asking for information, not evaluating or challenging it.

Confirming questions—"So, what you are saying is . . ."—
may be the most difficult to master, because the tone you use
sometimes can send unintended messages. A "Do you understand?" might be interpreted in the heat of the battle as, "Only a
dimwit wouldn't grasp this situation." Listen to yourself on tape
and assess your own vocal tones. What tones and phrasing suggest authentic concern?

- **Keep your promises with enraged customers.** If angry
  customers start using the phone as a weapon and erupt in
  a torrent of profanity, try saying, "I'm very sorry. I want
  to help, but I find your language upsetting. Can we try
  this again?" If that does not end the obscenity parade, go
  to a trump card: Hang up. That's right, end the call after
  some version of "I'd very much like to help, but I'm going to end the call if I continue to hear inappropriate language, and we can't find a better way to communicate."
  This action builds what is called "contractual trust"; you
  made a promise of action and followed through on it. In
  more cases than not, the customer will call back and apologize to you.
- **Let customers educate you.** When handling strange or
  unfamiliar problems with products or services, do not
  say, "I've just never heard of something like this before."
  Instead, respond with, "I don't mean to sound unin-
  formed, but can you tell me more about the problem?"
- **Transfer calls adeptly.** If you must transfer unhappy customers to a peer or manager, be clear in telling the customer the reason for the transfer—why you feel the need
  to pass on responsibility—and clearly state the name and
  title of the person the customer is being transferred to.
  Sloppy or seemingly uncaring transfers in these already
  tense situations can fan the flames of customer ire. Also,
  be sure you have the customer's name, company, and
  phone number in your company database or written
  down, in case the transfer does not work.
- **Make your listening "visible."** In face-to-face recovery
  situations, it is easy to give nonverbal clues that you are
  listening intently to the customer's problems: head nods,

direct eye contact, and the like. Not so over the phone. To make your listening more "visible," you need to use all phrases, such as "uh huh," "okay," and "mmm," that replace body gestures.

- **Discard command-and-control language.** Avoid saying "you'll need to" or "you'll have to" during phone interactions with an upset customer. That language implies a hierarchy of sorts or a master-and-servant relationship. Instead, practice using phrases such as, "I'd like to ask you to . . ." or "I think the best way to handle this might be . . ."
- **Do not use policy as a shield.** Irate customers will likely use a parroting of policy against you. Rather than saying, "Our policy won't allow that . . .," say, "Here's what I can do for you . . . ." Then state your policy or whatever is within your realm of recovery solutions.

For more tips on dealing with customers on the phone, see *Knock Your Socks Off Answers: Solving Customer Nightmares & Soothing Nightmare Customers.*

21

When and How to Fire a Customer

Business is a lot like tennis. Those who don't serve well end up losing.

—Hopson Scally

By now we know the customer is not always right, whether it is behavior that oversteps the bounds of civility, invalid claims, unreasonable demands, or out-and-out error or misjudgment. But owing to their status as the life blood of any organization—and to their standing as fellow human beings—customers *are* always worthy of fair and considerate treatment. Smart organizations focus on helping customers "discover" their own errors or misconceptions—gently as she goes—rather than rubbing their noses in it.

There will come times, however, when it is appropriate to go a step beyond and fire a customer. When the emotional or economical toll exacted from serving continually abusive or extremely high-maintenance, low-profit customers starts to outweigh the return on the investment, it is time to consider a customer exit strategy.

What often keeps us from lowering the boom on these highly toxic or bottom-line eroding customers, in addition to worries about replacing lost revenue, is the negative word of mouth we fear they will spread as a result of being fired. But that projection usually proves far worse in imagination than reality. People pay closest attention to word of mouth they perceive as credible and that comes from a reliable source. Chronic complainers do not typically carry the scarlet "C" mark of credibility. The desperately-in-need-of-firing customer more often than not is seen by others as perpetual victim and corrosive influence, and consequently their tales of woe and great injustice often are discounted by friends, colleagues, and even family.

When to Tell a Customer to "Hit the Road"

The challenge, of course, is deciding at what point the rewards of being without the customer outweigh the potential consequences of firing him. The price of saying "adios" includes the immediate loss of revenue as well as the aforementioned possibility of negative word of mouth. In such cases, it helps to remember that the payoff from customer firings will not necessarily be financial, at least not right away. Firing a customer who badly needs jettisoning sends a clear message to your people: You as manager will do whatever it takes to shield them from the fury and forces of misguided or inappropriate negative en-

ergy—energy that can keep them from serving other, better-behaved, or more profitable customers with the attention they deserve. The real dollar payoff comes when you replace that fired customer with one who is far easier to do business with and who does not drain your organization of the emotional, time, or monetary resources that often are in short supply to begin with.

Three Reasons to Fire Customers

Customers should be encouraged to exit for one of three reasons: They are costing you too much economically, they are costing you too much emotionally, or they are violating a key value of your organization.

- **Economic cost means profit.** Most organizations are in business to ensure that revenues adequately exceed expense. Not always at the outset, but over time. The credit card industry, for example, loses an average $80 in the first year of a relationship with a customer. Through advertising, marketing, sales, and solicitation expenses, there is always a "sunk cost" in acquiring customers. If there is not sufficient return on that initial investment over time, you will want to rethink whether a continued relationship makes sense. Where you draw the line depends on your own tolerance for red ink. Without a compelling reason to be tolerant, we would suggest you have none.
- **Emotional costs involve the wear and tear on your frontline associates.** Some customers are so taxing or abusive that the damage they do to employee self-esteem or everyday resilience robs you of fresh, enthusiastic people to effectively serve other, more deserving, or valuable customers. Do your employees perpetually complain about having to deal with one particularly abrasive or time-stealing customer? Have you witnessed repeated abuse of your people by a customer? When you occasionally ask employees to do something beyond the call of duty for particular clients, do you get resistance that feels out of

proportion to the request? If yes on any count, it may be time to consider favoring your employees' morale over a given customer's revenue contribution.

- **Clear violation of a key organizational value is the final reason to bid customers adieu.** This travels beyond morality or ethics infractions—consequences for such violations often are cut and dried—to include more nebulous values-based scenarios. If your reputation is built on responsiveness and you have a supplier whose chronic lateness is causing serious delays in your operation, for instance, it might warrant parting ways. Or if you are trying to build a progressive image in the marketplace and have some customers whose patronage does not suggest a cutting-edge presence, you might want to cut your loses and spend your service energy differently.

Whatever the conditions, make sure you have reasonably exhausted other options before cutting the customer cord. In some cases, you will find that special efforts can still "save" profitable but difficult customers on the verge of being fired. *Nation's Business* magazine reported on one such case at Consolidated Printing Co., a twenty-employee company in Chicago. The company's president, Marilyn Jones, was about to dismiss a customer because she was so difficult to work with. It was a big-dollar account, but the customer was "short tempered and nasty," Jones said. The customer clashed so often with a Consolidated rep that Jones decided to take over the account. She began by analyzing the customer's behavior and soon found this person was not secure in her job. "She didn't know how to spec a contract and wasn't willing to admit it," Jones told the magazine.

To turn the customer around, Jones figured she needed to educate her customer without making her feel like an imbecile. One thing she began doing was translating printing terms into more easily understandable language. "Glossy" paper became "shiny" paper, for instance.

With such hand holding over time, the difficult customer eventually turned into a more low-maintenance, less grating, and increasingly profitable Consolidated Printing client.

The Firing Act: Dos and Don'ts

Firing a customer is a bit like disarming a bomb. "Very carefully" is the operative term. The true goal is subduing animosity without scattering aftermath. Sometimes customers are so incensed at losing a favorite punching bag, even though it is actually you who has "lost" them, they can move quickly from anger to vindictiveness, seeking opportunities to punish, not just put down. You can limit your chances of such backlash by handling firings in cool-headed but still sensitive ways.

When Firing for Economic Reasons

Firing for an economic or bottom-line cause should always be rational, never emotional. Rational firings are laced with up-front motives and clearly spoken rationales, with emphasis on how a continued relationship will negatively affect the business, not on how a parting of ways will make your long-suffering staff feel like it has just won the Lotto. "Mr. Jones, we've greatly appreciated your business for the last year. We have elected to apply our limited resources in a new direction and will not be soliciting your business in the near future. Should you want to continue our relationship, it will likely need to be at a (higher price, greater volume, faster cycle time, lower cost, etc.)."

The goal is to cordially communicate that you can no longer justify a lose-win customer relationship, especially when the financial health of your business is at issue. You will want to be crystal clear on intent and speak with unequivocal conviction.

When Firing for Emotional or Values-Related Reasons

As furious, defensive, or protective as you may feel in these more emotionally charged firing situations, your rage will simply fuel the customer's own anger at being let go. Again, a rational explanation for why a continued relationship will harm your business—how harsh treatment of your service reps impairs productivity or how a difficult relationship steals time from other deserving customers—should be your modus operandi here.

If a customer firing is in defense of your associates or your values, it should also loudly say, "Stop . . . we do not tolerate your actions here." The goal is to give the customer a signal that he or she is unwelcome if the unwanted behavior persists. "Mrs. Jones, I must ask you to leave. The morale of our associates is critically important to their own well-being and to the well-being of our organization. And, although we are by no means perfect, our employees do not need to be repeatedly subjected to actions that demean them as people." The goal is not to send customers on an extended guilt trip, only to clearly state the facts and why continuing the relationship is not in the best interests of your organization.

Firing any customer, no matter how toxic or marginally profitable, might seem heresy in today's highly competitive markets, where companies fight tooth and nail—and often bleed out marketing or advertising budgets—for the attraction of new customers. Yet courageously ending relationships with customers who continually turn the blow torch on your front-line people or who, over time, siphon more funds from your bottom line than they return sends a message about who you are as a manager and what you stand for as an organization.

Appendix

How Ready Are You for Knock Your Socks Off Service Recovery When Things Go Wrong for Customers?

These self-assessment questions are adapted from the Service Management Practices Inventory™, a database of over 100 questions, and responses from over 80,000 managers and customer service employees in more than 400 companies, and from the Recovery Readiness Inventory™.

This is an opportunity for you to be as brutally frank and honest as you can stand being about your department's—or group's—shortcomings. At the same time, it is important to take credit for the good and right things you are already doing.

When you have completed the assessment, review your responses using the "Scoring Master" answer sheet (see page 207), then decide on appropriate improvement actions.

Systems, Policies, and Procedures

The extent to which our systems, policies, and procedures make it easy for front-line and support employees to deliver quality service in the face of a service breakdown and the degree to which systems, policies, and procedures are seen to support rather than inhibit good service recovery.

1. Assisting customers with problems is a clear priority in our company.

   ☐   Yes   ☐   No

2. The way my department/unit/division is organized makes it easy for employees to solve customer problems quickly.

   ☐   Yes   ☐   No

3. The way we are organized makes it easy for customers to reach the right individual or area when they have a problem or question.

   ☐   Yes   ☐   No

4. We provide a "service guarantee" to customers; it is well known among our customers.

   ☐   Yes   ☐   No

5. My department/unit/division has clearly defined procedures for what to do when mistakes are made or errors are discovered.

   ☐   Yes   ☐   No

6. Customers experiencing problems can start the recovery process with a single contact; our "system" does not require the customer to make multiple contacts to report a problem or get action.

   ☐   Yes   ☐   No

7. When problem solving takes longer than the initial contact, we have a system in place for staying in touch with the customer and updating him or her on the progress of the recovery process.

☐ Yes ☐ No

8. Front-line employees are allowed to make value-added "atonement" gestures, such as comping a repair or extending a subscription, at their own discretion.

☐ Yes ☐ No

9. All front-line and support employees know what they personally can do to solve customer problems.

☐ Yes ☐ No

10. When a customer problem is corrected, I am confident that it will not recur, at least not for this customer.

☐ Yes ☐ No

11. We have a formal process for collecting data on errors, complaints, and comments, analyzing their significance, and modifying our systems accordingly.

☐ Yes ☐ No

12. Our hiring criteria for front-line service people emphasizes "working with customer" skills as well as technical skills and knowledge.

☐ Yes ☐ No

Summary

My score on Systems, Policies, and Procedures: _____

Improvements I need to make:

_____

_____

_____

_____

_____

_____

Evaluating Service Performance

The degree to which we establish clear, customer-focused standards for service recovery and the extent to which we measure quality of work performance against those standards.

1. My department/unit/division has set clear standards for response time to customer complaints, questions, inquiries, and other contacts and correspondence.
   ☐ Yes ☐ No

2. Our standards are based on customer input rather than internally generated technical criteria.
   ☐ Yes ☐ No

3. We post our performance-to-standards data on a regular basis.
   ☐ Yes ☐ No

4. For us, regular means:
   ☐ Daily ☐ Weekly ☐ Monthly
   ☐ Quarterly ☐ Not At All

5. Everyone who works for me meets or exceeds those standards on a regular basis.
   ☐ Yes ☐ No

6. Our standards reflect "customer fixing" activities and outcomes as well as "problem fixing" activities and outcomes.
   ☐ Yes ☐ No

7. We ask customers to evaluate us on the results of every service recovery effort.
   ☐ Yes ☐ No

8. Customer evaluations include some elements of each of the following: reliability, assurance, tangibles, empathy, and responsiveness.
   ☐ Yes ☐ No

9. We "shop" and/or do "ride alongs" with service representatives on a regular basis (at least twice a year).
   ☐ Yes ☐ No

10. Some of our standards are tailored to specific customers with unique requirements.
    ☐ Yes ☐ No

Summary

My score on Evaluating Service Performance: _____

Improvements I need to make:

_____

_____

_____

_____

_____

Customer Focus and Commitment

The degree to which we as an organization, and our employees as individuals, think about, focus on, and are concerned with satisfying our customers on a day-to-day basis.

1. Employees feel empowered to take action to fulfill ordinary customer needs or solve unusual problems without special permission.
   ☐   Yes   ☐   No

2. Employees feel a personal sense of pride and ownership when they are able to use their service recovery skills to help customers.
   ☐   Yes   ☐   No

3. Employees are not afraid to ask customers about their satisfaction with our products and services; employees are comfortable acting on information about customer dissatisfaction.
   ☐   Yes   ☐   No

4. We make a policy of asking customers what they expect from us when problems occur.
   ☐   Yes   ☐   No

5. Our current standards are a result of asking customers what they expect of us when problem situations occur.
   ☐   Yes   ☐   No

6. There is good teamwork between individual employees and departments when solving customer problems.
   ☐   Yes   ☐   No

7. We almost always follow up with customers to be sure fixed problems stay fixed.
   ☐   Yes   ☐   No

8. It is not at all unusual to spot and solve potential customer problems before the customer is even aware of them.

☐   Yes   ☐   No

9. Everyone in my organization understands that retaining current customers through effective problem solving is every bit as important as gaining new customers.

☐   Yes   ☐   No

10. Everyone in my part of the organization knows the "dollars and sense" of customer retention.

☐   Yes   ☐   No

Summary

My score on Customer Focus and Commitment: _____

Improvements I need to make:

_____

_____

_____

_____

_____

Recognizing and Rewarding Service

The degree to which individual and group efforts to prevent, spot, and solve customer problems are recognized and rewarded in my department/unit/division.

1. Managers and supervisors in my department/unit/division constantly look for evidence of employees who take a personal interest in resolving customer complaints and problems.

   ☐   Yes   ☐   No

2. Such employees are frequently "spot" rewarded in a tangible way for their efforts.

   ☐   Yes   ☐   No

3. Employees who practice good service recovery are held up as role models for other employees.

   ☐   Yes   ☐   No

4. Employees who err working on behalf of a customer are confident that they will not be "punished."

   ☐   Yes   ☐   No

5. Employees know that their ability to prevent, spot, and solve customer problems plays an important part in performance reviews and advancement decisions.

   ☐   Yes   ☐   No

6. We have a formal system that allows employees to recognize and thank other employees for their assistance in solving a customer's problem.

   ☐   Yes   ☐   No

7. We have a formal system that encourages our customers to recognize employees for the assistance in preventing or correcting a service breakdown.

   ☐   Yes   ☐   No

Summary

My score on Recognizing and Rewarding Service: _____

Improvements I need to make:

_____

_____

_____

_____

_____

Training and Coaching

The degree to which employees are trained and coached to do what is necessary to meet customers' needs and solve customers' problems.

1. We encourage employees to go "above and beyond" for customers.

   ☐   Yes   ☐   No

2. Employees believe that their "above and beyond" efforts for customers are recognized and valued.

   ☐   Yes   ☐   No

3. We train customer contact people in the "how to's" of:
   - Listening carefully and fully to customers
   - "Reading" customer types and/or moods
   - Making a positive impression during problem fixing
   - Dealing with angry customers

4. We take specific actions to help employees deal with the stress that comes from customer contact.

   ☐   Yes   ☐   No

5. When an employee does not feel capable of dealing with a particular customer or customer problem, he or she knows exactly whom to ask for assistance.

   ☐   Yes   ☐   No

6. Managers and supervisors in my department/unit/division regularly meet one on one with employees to coach them on service recovery skills.

   ☐   Yes   ☐   No

7. Employees regularly meet together—without a manager present—to discuss "tough" customer problems and to exchange information on solving customer problems.

   ☐   Yes   ☐   No

Summary

My score on Training and Coaching: _____

Improvements I need to make:

_____

_____

_____

_____

How Ready Are You to Recover When Things Go Wrong for Customers? Scoring Master

Systems, Policies, and Procedures		Evaluating Service Performance		Customer Focus and Commitment		Recognizing and Rewarding Service		Training and Coaching	
Yes	No	Yes	No	Yes	No	Yes	No	Yes	No
1. 2	0	1. 3	0	1. 3	0	1. 2	0	1. 3	0
2. 3	0	2. 2	0	2. 2	0	2. 2	0	2. 2	0
3. 3	0	3. 2	0	3. 2	0	3. 2	0	3. A = 2, B = 1, C = 2, D = 3 Max = 8	
4. 2	0	4. 2 for D/M/W 1 for Q		4. 3	0	4. 2	0	4. 2	0
5. 3	0	5. 3	0	5. 2	0	5. 3	0	5. 2	0
6. 2	0	6. 2	0	6. 3	0	6. 2	0	6. 2	0
7. 2	0	7. 2 for *Every* 1 for *Majority*		7. 2	0	7. 2	0	7. 2	0
8. 2	0	8. 2 for all 5 1 for 3 of 5		8. 2	0				
9. 2	0			9. 1	0				
10. 3	0	9. 2	0	10. 1	0				
11. 2	0	10. 3	0						
12. 2	0								
28	0	21	0	21	0	15	0	21	0
Minimum Comfort Zone: 22		Minimum Comfort Zone: 16		Minimum Comfort Zone: 16		Minimum Comfort Zone: 12		Minimum Comfort Zone: 12	

RECOVERY REPORT CARD

91–106	A+	80–84	B+
85–90	A	75–79	B

Less than 79 points: "Not any worse than anybody else— and not any better."

Afterword

In the quest to provide high-quality, cutting-edge, customer-pleasing products and services, errors do occasionally happen through no fault of the customer or provider, and they have a significant impact on customer retention. But regardless of the source of an error, a customer is involved and a customer is at risk because of the error. Service recovery is a process designed to save the at-risk customer and, secondarily, to feed useful information for problem prevention back into an organization's quality management and quality assurance processes.

In summary, our key points are as follows:

1. Recovery, or returning an aggrieved customer to a state of satisfaction after a service or product breakdown, has a critical economic impact on your business.
2. Breakdown involves customer expectations of both outcomes and processes.
3. Recovering well when things have gone wrong increases customer loyalty and decreases marketing expenses.
4. Only your customer can tell you how annoying or victimizing a particular service breakdown has been. Only your customer can determine when appropriate recovery has occurred.
5. Planned service recovery ensures that each breakdown is handled creatively and satisfies customer and organizational needs.
6. You can—and should—plan for the unexpected.
7. When problems occur, customers expect you to apologize, give them a fair fix, treat them like you care, and atone for injuries.
8. "Fix the person, then the problem" is a good rule unless you cannot fix the problem. Planned recovery helps you do both—and do them well.
9. It is critical to identify recurring problems so that you can make changes and corrections in production and service delivery systems.

10. Planned service recovery improves overall service quality awareness and motivates employees to work on the customer's behalf to solve problems.

Creating service quality is a journey, not a destination. In our competitive world, customer expectations constantly change and rise, due, in part, to the never-ending contest to be first in the customer's esteem and first in the marketplace. Service recovery, done well, energizes the effort to create quality service and motivates service employees to "keep on keepin' on" on the customer's behalf. Done right, service recovery tells the customer "we're here to set things right when they go wrong. No problem." William James, the father of American psychology, commented that "the deepest principle of human nature is a craving to be appreciated." That is true of our customers, true of our peers, and true of our associates. And nothing is more appreciated that a problem solved faster, easier, and more effectively than a customer dared hope.

Additional Resources

To assist you with your lifelong learning, here is a list of resources that you may find helpful. As more resources become available, this might be a good place to add new favorites.

Anderson, Kristin, and Ron Zemke. *Coaching Knock Your Socks Off Service.* New York: AMACOM, 1997.

Anderson, Kristin, and Ron Zemke. *Delivering Knock Your Socks Off Service, 2nd Edition.* New York: AMACOM, 1998.

Anderson, Kristin, and Ron Zemke. *Knock Your Socks Off Answers: Solving Customer Nightmares & Soothing Nightmare Customers.* New York: AMACOM, 1995.

Bell, Chip R. *Beep! Beep! Competing in the Age of the Road Runner.* New York: Warner, 2000.

Bell, Chip R. *Customers As Partners: Building Relationships That Last.* San Francisco: Berrett Koehler, 1994.

Bell, Chip R. *Managers As Mentors: Building Partnerships for Learning.* San Francisco: Berrett Koehler, 1996.

Bell, Chip R., and Ron Zemke. *Managing Knock Your Socks Off Service.* New York: AMACOM, 1992.

Berry, Leonard. *Discovering the Soul of Service.* New York: The Free Press, 1999.

Connellan, Thomas K., and Ron Zemke. *Sustaining Knock Your Socks Off Service.* New York: AMACOM, 1993.

Connellan, Thomas K. *Inside the Magic Kingdom: Seven Keys to Disney's Success.* Dallas: Bard Press, 1997.

Woods, John, and Ron Zemke. *Best Practices in Customer Service.* New York: AMACOM, 1998.

Zemke Ron. *The Service Edge: 101 Companies that Profit from Customer Care.* New York: New American Library, 1989.

About the Authors

Ron Zemke is a management consultant and researcher who has become one of the best-known and most widely quoted authorities on the continuing service revolution. As senior editor of *TRAINING* magazine and a syndicated columnist, he has covered the emergence and development of the global service economy. Ron has authored or co-authored twenty-five books, including the seven-book *Knock Your Socks Off Service* series, and *Generations At Work*. In 1994 he was given the MOBIUS award by the Society of Consumer Affairs Professionals, and in 1995 was named one of the New Quality Gurus by *Quality Digest Magazine*. Ron travels the globe sharing with organizations the importance of developing strong relationships with customers and the long-term value and impact retaining those customer relationships can have to the bottom line.

Chip R. Bell is a senior principal with Performance Research Associates and manages their Dallas, Texas office. Prior to joining the firm in the mid-1980s, he was Vice President and Director of Management and Organizational Development for NCNB (now BankAmerica). He is the author or co-author of twelve books, including *Customers as Partners, Managers as Mentors, Dance Lessons: Six Steps to Great Partnerships in Business and Life, Beep Beep! Competing in the Age of the Road Runner,* and *Managing Knock Your Socks Off Service*. An internationally renowned speaker, Dr. Bell has worked with several Fortune 500 companies, including IBM, Cadillac, USAA, Microsoft, Lucent Technologies, MCI WorldCom, Lockheed Martin, Harley-Davidson, Marriott, 3M, Nortel, State Farm, Merrill Lynch, Ritz-Carlton Hotels, and Victoria's Secret.

Performance Research Associates is one of North America's premier customer relationship management consulting firms, specializing in helping organizations develop a customer-centric perspective. Performance Research Associates has offices in Minneapolis, Dallas, Ann Arbor, and Orlando, providing training and consulting services to clients in North America, Europe, South America, and along the Pacific Rim. The *Knock Your Socks Off Service* series draws on the experience and work of the partners of Performance Research Associates. Readers interested in information about presentations, consulting, or other Performance Research Associates services may contact the firm's Minneapolis office at (800) 359-2576 or at pra@socksoff.com.